WELCOME TRAVEL GUIDE

MALTA and GOZO
Sun, Sea and History

The Auberge de Castille, Valletta, re-built in 1744

WELCOME TRAVEL GUIDE

MALTA and GOZO

Sun, Sea and History

John Manduca

with watercolours by
Cecily Napier

Publishers Enterprises Group (PEG) Ltd

Published by
Publishers Enterprises Group (PEG) Ltd,
P.E.G. Building
UB7, Industrial Estate,
San Gwann SGN 09, Malta

http://www.peg.com.mt
E-mail: contact@peg.com.mt

© John Manduca, 2003

All rights reserved. No part of this publication may be reproduced, stored in a retrieval system or transmitted in any form or by any means, electronic, mechanical, photocopying, recording, or otherwise, without prior permission in writing of the author and the publishers.

First published as
Tourist Guide to Malta & Gozo, 1975
Seventh (revised) edition, 1980

Revised and enlarged and first published as
Welcome Travel Guide: Malta and Gozo, 2003

ISBN: 99909-0-337-9

By the same author

Welcome Travel Guide: City of Mdina and Rabat (2003)
Harbours of Malta (1974)
Malta Who's Who 1987
Antique Maltese Clocks (Ed.) (1992)
The Palace of the Grand Masters (Ed.) (2001) (Prize-Winner)
Antique Furniture in Malta (Ed.) (2002)
Treasures of Malta (Ed.) (1994–   )

Printed by PEG Ltd, Malta

For
SYLVIA,
and
ANNE, MARTIN, LOUISE
and
ANTHONY

Know you the land where the lemon trees bloom?
Where the gold orange flows in the deep thicket's gloom;
Where a wind ever soft from the blue heaven blows,
And the groves are of laurel and myrtle and rose?
Do you know it well?
There, there I would go, O my beloved with you.

GOETHE

Acknowledgments

I have tested the patience of my friends and colleagues in putting this travel guide together.

Leonard Zammit Munro and other officials of the Malta Tourism Authority have been most helpful with information and photographs.

I am deeply indebted to Cecily Napier for her watercolours which give the guide a distinctive character.

The maps of Malta and of Gozo are by the Survey and Planning Unit of the Malta Environment and Planning Authority, Floriana. The other twelve plans are by Polidano Press Ltd; these should help you find your way around.

Thanks are due to the publishers PEG Ltd for their encouragement.

My wife, Sylvia, together with our children, have shown a great deal of forbearance. My son Martin spent long hours proof-reading. My grandchildren came to the rescue when my computer became temperamental, which was quite often.

I have tried to include anything which is attractive or relevant to the visitor or the temporary resident, and have tried to ensure accuracy; although one should be aware that things have a tendency to change or to disappear; standards sometimes improve and they sometimes deteriorate.

The front cover and photographs Nos. 3, 24, 37 and 48 are by Fr Michael Fsadni O.P.; Nos. 1, 9, 18 and 39 come courtesy of the Malta Tourism Authority; Kevin Casha provided the frontispiece as well as the photographs on the back cover, and Nos 2, 3, 15, 20, 21, 22, 23, 26, 27, 30, 32,

35, 39, 41, 43, 44, 45, 46 and 47; Nos. 4, 5, 7, 8, 10, 11, 12, 13, 14, 29, 33, 34 and 36 come courtesy of *Fondazzjoni Patrimonju Malti*; No. 5 courtesy of Papas Borgia; No. 12 is courtesy of Alvin Scicluna; No 16 courtesy of Mark A. Vella and 'Malta at War'; No. 26 is by the Malta Environment and Planning Authority; while the remainder are by the author.

The Publishers and I welcome your comments, additions and corrections, for possible inclusion in subsequent editions of this WELCOME TRAVEL GUIDE.

Thank you.

The Author

RATING

This book is user friendly and employs a simple rating system to help you choose which places to visit when time is short.

- ✠✠✠   *Top attraction – Do not miss*
- ✠✠   *Highly Recommended*
- ✠   *Well-Worth visiting*

PRICES

Where appropriate, an indication of the approximate cost of a three-course meal is given by the £ sign.

£££ denotes higher prices; ££ average prices; and £ denotes lower charges.

* * *

Every effort has been made to ensure accuracy throughout the WELCOME GUIDE at the time of going to Press. However, descriptions, assessments and prices tend to change; establishments also change hands.

Contents

List of Illustrations 17

A Word of Introduction 23

On Arrival – *What you need to know* 25

History in Brief – *Visitors through the Ages* 31

What to See (1) – *Valletta's Streets of Palaces* 43
A Look Around 46
Museum of Fine Arts 47
National Museum of Archaeology 48
St John's Co-Cathedral 48
The Museum of St John 53
National Library of Malta (*Bibliotheca*) 54
Other Libraries 55
"The Great Siege" 55
The Palace 55
The Tapestry Chamber 58
The Armoury 58
Casa Rocca Piccola 59
The Manoel Theatre 59
The Auberges 60
St Paul's Anglican Church 62
St Paul Shipwrecked Church 62
"Our Lady of Damascus" 64
Fort St Elmo 65
War Museum 66
"La Vittoria" 66

9

"Il-Monti" 68
Jesuit Church 68
Mediterranean Conference Centre 69
"The Malta Experience" 70
The Siege Bell Memorial 70
Lascaris War Rooms 71

Sliema and St Julians 71

What to See (2) – *Mdina – Proud City* 89
Natural History Museum 91
St Agatha's Chapel 92
Nunnery of St Benedict 92
Casa Inguanez 93
Banca Giuratale 94
The Cathedral 94
Catheral Museum 97
Chapel of St Roque 97
Our Lady of Mount Carmel 98
The 'Norman House' 98
Bastion Square 99
Chapel of St Nicholas 99

What to See (3) – *Rabat and Beyond* 101
Roman House and Museum 101
Casa Bernard 101
St Paul's Church and Grotto 104
Wignacourt College Museum 105
St Paul's Catacombs 107
St Agatha's Catacombs 107
Santo Spirito Hospital 108
St Dominic's Priory and Church 108
Verdala Castle 109
Inquisitor's Summer Palace 110
Dingli Cliffs 111

What to See (4) – *Prehistoric Sites and Temples* ... 121
The Hypogeum (*Hal Saflieni*) 121

Tarxien Temples and Museum 123
Ħaġar Qim and Mnajdra Temples 123
Għar Dalam 125
Cart-Ruts 125
Prehistoric Cultural Sequence 127

What to See (5) – *Forts and Fortifications* 129
The Knights and the British 129
British Fortifications 134
Fort Rinella 134
In Gozo 135

What to See (6) – *Gardens and Garden Centres* 136
Upper Baracca 136
The Lower Baracca 137
Hastings Gardens 137
The Mall – Floriana 138
Argotti – Floriana 139
Sa Maison – Floriana 139
Garden of Repose – Floriana 141
San Anton Palace and Gardens – Attard 142
Buskett – Outskirts of Rabat 143
Kennedy Memorial Grove – Salina 143
Palazzo Parisio – Naxxar 144
The Chinese Garden of Serenity – Santa Lucia 144
Rundle Gardens – Victoria, Gozo 144
Cemeteries 145
Garden Centres 146

What to See (7) – *In the Footsteps of St Paul* 149
St Paul's Grotto 149
The Sanctuary at Mellieħa 150
St Paul's Island 152
The Cathedral in Mdina 153
The Parish Church in Rabat 153
The Anglican Cathedral in Valletta 153

***What to See (8)** – Grand Harbour and Vittoriosa*............ 167
St Angelo 170
Inquisitor's Palace 171
Church of St Lawrence 172
The first Auberges 173
The Maritime Museum 173
Villa Bighi at Kalkara 174
Exhibition Hall 175

Other Places of Interest 176
Buġibba and Qawra 176
Mosta Church 176
Wied Iż-Żurrieq – The Blue Grotto 177
Siġġiewi – "Heritage in Stone" 179
Malta Aviation Museum, Ta' Qali 179
Ħal Millieri Mediaeval Chapel 179
Ħal Far – Ħasan's Cave 181
Għadira Nature Reserve 181

Off the Beaten Track 182
Cliffs and Countryside 182
Walks and Excursions 185

Island of Gozo 190
The Castello (The Citadel) 193
The Cathedral 193
St George's Basilica 195
The Museums 195
Victoria (Rabat) 196
Ġgantija Temples 196
Ta' Pinu Basilica 197
The Xewkija Rotunda 198
Stalactite Caves 199
Qawra and Dwejra 199
Fungus Rock 201
18th Century Windmills 201

Museums	202
Where to Swim	202
The Library	203
Walking in Gozo	203
Practical Information	204
Transport	206
Little Comino	207

Where to Stay 220

What and Where to Eat 227
Local Dishes 227
Fish 228
Wine 229
Beer 229
Cheese 229
Fruit 229
Delicious Bread 229
Water 230
Restaurants (Malta) 230
Restaurants (Gozo) 237

Entertainment 238
Theatre 238
Ice Ring 238
Gambling 239
Cinema 239
Television 240
Disco – Nightclubs 240
Audio Visual Shows 240
Keeping Children Amused 242
Traditions and Crafts of Malta 243

A Note on Shopping 244
Shopping Centres 244
Things to Look For 244
Open Air Markets 247
Chemists 247

13

Swimming and other Sports 249
Swimming 249
Other Sports 251

Harbour Cruises – *Tour of the Harbours* 253
Marsamxett Harbour 253
Grand Harbour 254

Mediterranean Climate 255
Weather Lore 257
Points of the Compass 258

Half-Day Excursions 259
Licensed Guides 260

Hints for the Motorist 261
Distances from Valletta 262
Distances from Victoria (Gozo) 263
Distances from Mġarr (Gozo) 263
Petrol Stations 264
Traffic Accidents 264
Timed Parking Zone 264

Festas and Festivals 265
Festas 265
Blessing of Animals 266
Good Friday 267
The Last Supper 267
Easter Sunday 267
Christmas 268
The "Imnarja" 268
Carnival 268
Freedom Day, Independence Day and
 Republic Day 269
Feast of Our Lady of Victories (8th September) 269
Trade Fair 269

CONTENTS

Of Things Maltese 270
Karrozzin – Horse-Drawn Cab 270
The *Dghajsa* – Taxi-boat 271
Brass Dolphins – Door-knockers 271
Hand-made Lace 272
The Blood Orange 272
The Maltese Dog 273
The Wall Clock – "Arloġġ ta' Malta" 274
The Faldetta – Head-dress 275
Wooden Balconies 275

Ancient Customs 278
First Birthday 278
Carnival 278
Folklore 279
Weather Lore 280

Facts at Your Fingertips 281
Bus Service 281
Museums at a Glance 283
Banks 284
Public Holidays 285
Airline Agents 286
Posts, Telephones and Telegrams 287
'Mobile Guide' 288
Taxi Fares 288
Newspapers 289
Hospitals 289
Nursing 289
Tourist Information Services 289
Learning English 290
Cultural Activities 290
Useful Telephone Numbers 292
Sunday Church Services 293
The Language – "Malti" 297
Embassies/Diplomatic Representation in Malta 299

15

Further Reading 303

Appendices 305
Sovereigns from 1090 to 1530 305
Grand Masters of the Order of St John in Malta 307
Governors and Governors-General 308
Presidents 310
Prime Ministers of Malta 311

Index 313

List of Illustrations

Watercolours

St John's Co-Cathedral, Valletta 50
The Palace of the Grand Masters 56
Auberge de Castille 61
Valletta skyline 63
Our Lady of Victories Church 67
Main Gate, *Città Vecchia* 90
Palazzo Vilhena, *Città Vecchia* 91
The Metropolitan Cathedral, Mdina 95
Statue of St Paul in the Grotto, Rabat 104
Wignacourt Museum, Rabat 106
Verdala Castle 110
The temple at *Ħaġar Qim* 124
Senglea 130
Wignacourt Tower, St Paul's Bay 132
The Red Tower, Mellieha 132
De Redin coastal tower 133
Sarria Church, Floriana 139
President's Palace, San Anton, Attard 142
St Paul's Island 151
The fishing 'luzzu' 152
The Castle of St Angelo 171
Maritime Museum, Vittoriosa 174
The 'Rotunda' Church at Mosta 175
The Blue Grotto, Żurrieq 176
Medieval Chapel of *Ħal Millieri* 180
A wayside Chapel 183
Medieval Chapel of *Bir Miftuħ* 188

17

The Citadel, Gozo 192
The Cathedral, Gozo... 194
Ġgantija Temple 197
Dwejra, Gozo 199
Ta' Pinu Church 200
Comino Island.. 207
Village of Marsaxlokk 236
Għajn Tuffieħa Bay... 250
The 'Karozzin' 270
The 'Dgħajsa' 271

Photographs

Frontispiece: Auberge de Castille................................ 2
1. The Co-Cathedral of St John, described by William Thackeray, the novelist, as 'magnificent' 72
2. A detail of the Madonna and Child from the mausoleum of Ramon Perellos – a splendid Baroque monument in white marble 73
3. The Grand Harbour from Valletta; the Armoury at the Palace 74
4. The Mediterranean Conference Centre, formerly the Hospital of the Knights................................... 75
5. A statue in Carrera marble of Queen Victoria (1834-1901), the work of Giuseppe Valenti, to mark the Monarch's Jubilee..................................... 76
6. The Anglican pro-Cathedral, built at the expense of the Dowager Queen Adelaide of England in 1840; the National Library built in 1786................. 77
7. One of the Gobelin tapestries in the Palace of the Grand Masters – a gift of Grand Master Perellos y Roccaful (1697-1720).. 78
8. The Manoel Theatre built in 1731 and claimed to be the second oldest theatre still in use in Europe 79

LIST OF ILLUSTRATIONS

9. A scene from the frescoes depicting the Great Siege of 1565, painted by Matteo Perez d'Aleccio in 1601 80
10. Ancient icon of Our Lady of Damascus, brought to Malta from Rhodes in 1530 and venerated in the Greek Catholic Church 81
11. The Museum of Fine Arts in South Street, Valletta; one of the sculptures on display – *Arab Horses*, by Maltese artist Antonio Sciortino (1879-1947) 82
12. The Palace of the Grand Masters – the main entrance to the Armoury in the 18th century 83
13. A painting by Antoine Favray (1706-1798) showing Maltese costumes and a Maltese Wall Clock in the background, at the Museum of Fine Arts 84
14. 'The Adoration of the Magi', one of a set of magnificent Flemish Tapestries woven after paintings by Peter Paul Rubens (1577-1620) at the Museum of St John's Cathedral 85
15. Senglea from Valletta; Fort St Angelo on guard in Grand Harbour 86
16. The War Memorial in Floriana; Queen Victoria surveys the devastation of war – the Palace in Valletta is on the right 87
17. Aerial view of the old Capital City; a 19th century painting of Mdina by the Schranz Brothers 112
18. The Metropolitan Cathedral in Mdina 113
19. The Arms of Grand Master Vilhena on the façade; the patron Saints of Mdina – St Publius, St Paul and St Agatha – on the inside of the entrance to the City 114
20. The Tower of the Standard at the entrance to the city 115
21. The Main Gate to Mdina; *Città Vecchia* by night ... 116

19

22. Sunset over the 'City of all Time' 117
23. Parish Church of St Paul in Rabat 118
24. The splendid cloister at St Dominic's Priory; The Catacombs in Rabat 119
25. Palazzo Vilhena by night 120
26. An effigy of St Paul at the entrance to Mdina 154
27. Maltese sunset – "Golden Glow" 155
28. The Temple of Mnajdra dating back to 2800BC; The Hypogeum – one of the wonders of the world 156
29. Aerial view of the temple of Ħaġar Qim, one of the statuettes found during excavations at the Brocktorff Circle in Xagħra, Gozo 157
30. The temple of Ġgantija in Gozo – older than Stonehenge and the Pyramids of Egypt; the mysterious cart-ruts scattered all over the island ... 158
31. Striking aerial view of the Citadel in Gozo 159
32. Entrance to Fort Ricasoli at the mouth of Grand Harbour, built in 1694 160
33. Mosta church with its mighty dome claimed to be the third largest in the world 161
34. Portes des Bombes, Floriana; the Courve Porte, Vittoriosa 162
35. Żabbar Gate, Cottonera 163
36. Courtyard, Inquisitor's Palace, Vittoriosa 164
37. The garden at San Anton; one of several garden centres 165
38. Aerial view of the Grand Harbour with Valletta, Fort Ricasoli, Fort St Angelo and Senglea 166
39. Fishing nets 209
40. The Cathedral, said to have been built between 1697 and 1711 on a site once used as a temple to a Phoenician goddess; an old print of the Fungus Rock at Dwejra Bay, Gozo 210
41. Victoria (Rabat), Gozo; Ta' Pinu Basilica in Għarb, Gozo 211

42. The courtyard in the Capuchin Friary,
    Victoria, Gozo 212
43. Sandy beach at Għajn Tuffieħa Bay, Malta; a
    secluded beach at Daħlet Qorrot, Gozo 213
44. The Blue Lagoon, Comino; fishing boats in
    Marsalforn, Gozo 214
45. Wied il-Għasri, Gozo 215
46. Diving 216
47. Sailing 217
48. The Roman Apiary at Xemxija; the Chinese
    'Garden of Serenity' at Santa Lucia 218
49. The sun sets over St Paul's Bay 219
50. A Maltese wall clock 276
51. An oil painting of a Chicken Hawker by
    Edward Caruana Dingli (1876-1950) 277

Maps and Plans

Malta .... *inside front cover*
Valletta 44-45
St John's Co-Cathedral 49
Mdina 88
Rabat 102-103
Archaeological Sites and Temples 122
Forts and Fortifications 128
Vittoriosa (Birgu) 168-169
Margherita and Cotoner Lines 184
Victoria and The Citadel 190
Sliema and St Julians 222-223
Swimming and Diving 248
Malta Bus Routes 282
Gozo .... *inside back cover*

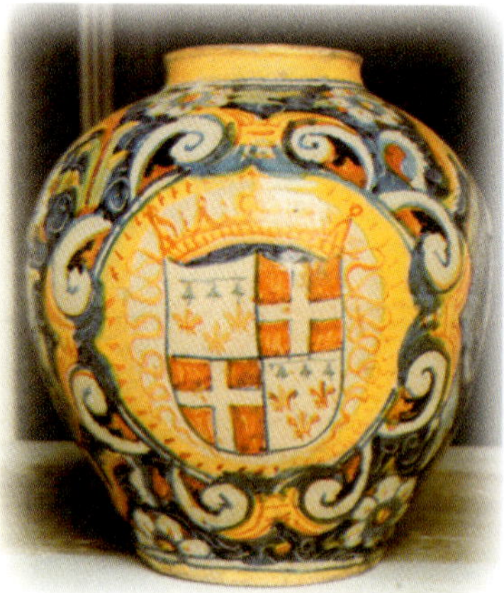

A Word of Introduction

Malta is a fascinating place. So is Gozo. To get the best out of them you need a little time and most visitors have not a great deal at their disposal.

The purpose of this illustrated WELCOME TRAVEL GUIDE to Malta and Gozo is to help you to get around, see all you want to see and enjoy yourself with the minimum of effort. It aims at being an up-to-date practical guide book which you can handle easily.

I have tried to include all the information which a visitor likes to have at his or her fingertips. And I have tried to do this as concisely and attractively as possible. Fourteen maps and plans should help you around and, hopefully, prevent you from getting lost. The delightful watercolours by Cecily Napier will give added pleasure; so should the ninety or so photographs.

There is much in the Maltese Islands which is of interest to the lover of art and architecture, the historian and the archaeologist. More and more people are becoming aware of our heritage and of the need to safeguard the environment before more damage is done.

Malta is three hours flight from London and under two hours from Rome. The sun shines much of the time; the sea is blue and inviting. And most people understand English.

This is a small friendly country with a long and chequered history. There is much to see and do – if that is what you want. You may prefer to laze in the Mediterranean sun. Either way I hope you enjoy yourself.

"Beaulieu", Mdina *(Città Vecchia)*

April, 2003   JOHN MANDUCA

On Arrival

What you need to know

Travellers sometimes lose their bearings. A Turkish Admiral on reconnaissance late in the 16th century reported that Malta had disappeared. Four hundred years later the Axis Powers were to make similar claims. Both were wrong. For the record, Malta is the largest of a group of Islands in the centre of the Mediterranean, with Sicily 97 kilometres to the north and the mainland of Africa some 322 kilometres to the South. On the tip of southern Europe, it is equidistant from the eastern and western ends of the Mediterranean. The Island is 27.50 kilometres long and 14.50 kilometres wide and Gozo, Comino, Cominotto and Filfla are the other islands making up the Maltese archipelago[1]. All in all, about the size of the Isle of Wight. So much for geography.

Now lets get down to the business on hand.

You come in either by plane through Malta International Airport at Gudja or by boat and land in Valletta, the capital, where one cannot fail to notice the attractively painted *dgħajsa* (a taxi-boat, pronounced "dyesah"). In either case your first encounter will be with

---

[1] Cominotto and Filfla are tiny and uninhabited. The total area of the three islands is 316 square kilometres (Malta 246, Gozo 67, Comino 2.7). The total population is just under 400,000.

passport, immigration and customs officials, porters, taxi drivers and the like. What follows should help to make these encounters relatively painless.

Passports

If you are staying for three months or less this is all you need. If you are staying longer you should apply to the Administrative Secretary, Office of the Prime Minister, Valletta.

Visas

If you are from the United Kingdom, Commonwealth countries, members of the Council of Europe, the United States of America or Japan you do not need a visa.

Customs

Items for personal use are not liable to duty. Cigars and tobacco (in reasonable quantities) are allowed in free. You are also allowed 200 cigarettes and one bottle of spirits, and one of wine without payment of duty. (Importation of drugs or pornography is not allowed and may lead to trouble with the law).

Health

Visitors from Europe, the United States, Canada and Australia do not require certificates of vaccination or inoculation.

Currency

The islands' currency is decimal. A Maltese *Lira* (written as Lm) is equal to 100 cents. Notes are to the value of Lm20,

Lm10, Lm5 and Lm2. Coins are issued in denominations of Lm1, 50c, 25c, 10c, 5c, 2c and 1 cent. The amount of Maltese currency that may be brought in is Lm50.

Most international credit cards are accepted and ATMs are to be found in most towns.

Banks

The leading Banks are HSBC, the Bank of Valletta, Lombard Bank and APS. Opening hours are usually 8.30 a.m. to 12.45 p.m., Monday to Friday, and from 8.30 a.m. to 12 noon on Saturday. Exchange facilities are available at the airport. Exchange rates may be obtained by dialling free phone 0800 773322.

Taxis

Taxis tend to be on the expensive side and fares have an unfortunate habit of varying. Despite meters you are advised to ask the taxi-driver what he intends charging before stepping into his cab (painted white) (see page 288).

Driving a Car

Drive on the left and drive carefully. You need a valid driving licence. Driving signs are in English. At present lead-reduced petrol (LRP) costs 38 cents a litre, while unleaded petrol costs 35 cents.

By Bus

The Bus service is inexpensive though not always comfortable. For information on bus services, telephone 212259916. All towns and villages are linked to the terminus at the City Gate, Valletta. Routes are identified by number (see pages 281-282).

Where to Stay (see pages 220)

What and where to Eat (see page 227)

Language

No difficulty. Maltese and English are both official languages and most people speak or understand English. If you wish to show off your knowledge of Maltese all you need to learn is "Grazzi ħafna" which means "thank you very much"; and "Saħħa"[2] (literally, "health") which is used to say "good-bye" or "au revoir". The Maltese language is structurally Semitic and has absorbed many words of Romance origin, mainly Italian (see page 297).

Climate

On the whole, excellent. Fog, snow and frost are unknown. Rain averages 22ins (558mm) in a whole year, and when it comes it usually does so in short heavy showers. The *average* temperature for winter (November-April) is 13.7°C (56.6°F) and for summer 22.6°C (72.7°F). The *average* daily sunshine for winter is 6.1 hours and for summer 10.6 hours (see page 255).

Clothing

Warm clothing is recommended for December, January and February; lighter wear for March, April, May, October and November; and very light wear for June, July, August

---

[2] "Saħħa" had found its way into *The Concise Oxford Dictionary*.

> **The Language Question**
>
> Italian was an offical language until 1934 when it was replaced by Maltese which, alongside English, was recognized for the first time as an 'official language', after a prolonged political dispute which divided the island for many years.

and September. A light raincoat may come in useful from October to March.

Bathing

The bathing season extends from May to October when the sea temperature averages 22.7°C (73°F). (see pages 249-250).

Shopping

Most shops are open between 9 a.m. and 7 p.m. (8 p.m. on Saturday) with a two hours break for lunch (see pages 244-245).

Licensing Hours

Bars, Cafés and restaurants are normally open between 9 a.m. and midnight, 4 a.m. for discos. You can get a drink any time during these hours.

Tipping

Tips are expected in restaurants and hotels and by taxi drivers. There are no fixed rules and commonsense should prevail. 10% on bills is reasonable. Car park attendants are usually given 15c-25c.

Religion

Roman Catholic. The Constitution guarantees freedom of conscience and worship to all denominations. (see page 291).

Electricity

240 volts – single phase – 50 cycles.

Time

The time in the Maltese Islands is one hour ahead of G.M.T. (Two hours ahead during Summer-time – between the last Sunday in March and the last Sunday in October).

Post and Telephones (see pages 286-287)

Links with Home: Embassies (see page 299-301)

Further Information

In Malta. The Government Tourist Information Service, 1 City Gate Arcade, Valletta (Tel. 21237747) and Malta Tourism Authority, Merchants Street, Valletta (Tel. 21224444).

In London. Tourist Information Centre, Malta House, Malta High Commission 36-38 Piccadilly (Tel. 2772924800).

History in Brief

Visitors through the Ages

The Maltese Islands are steeped in history and whether or not you agree with Henry Ford's celebrated remark that "history is bunk", an outline of the Island's history is necessary if you are to enjoy and appreciate your stay here to the full. In any case, once you are here it is interesting to know something about those who came before you.

The first visitor to our shores was probably Neanderthal Man, but little is known about him and it is safest to advance rapidly many thousand of years into the Stone Age. The men of this age were great builders and the thirty or so temples and underground sanctuaries, which they left behind them in Malta and Gozo, are evidence of their strength and their skill. These awesome temples are the earliest freestanding monuments of stone in the world. They predate Stonehenge and the great pyramids of Egypt (see pages 121-127).

Myth has it that Jason and his band of Argonauts tried to seek shelter here in a storm but failed to make it because of the failing light; that Dido's sister Anna, fleeing from her enemies was given asylum in the "fruitful isle of Malta" by King Battus, King of Malta; and that Ulysses was cast ashore and remained seven years with the nymph Calypso. Be that as it may, the history of Malta properly begins with the Phoenicians who came around 1450 B.C. and started a fashion which was followed by the Carthaginians, possibly

the Greeks, the Romans, the Arabs, the Normans, the Swabians, The Angevins, the Aragonese, the Castilians, the Order of St John of Jerusalem, the French and, for 164 years, the British. In September 1964, Malta became an independent State within the Commonwealth only to be occupied again soon after by the present day tourist.
We will take them in turn.

The Phoenicians (1450-550 B.C.)

A seafaring people who sailed as far as Cornwall in England in search of tin, they found refuge here in their purple-sailed galleys and called the island "Maleth" which means shelter. Excellent traders, sailors and explorers, they soon got down to business and the Maltese Islands were regarded as among the more prosperous of the Phoenician colonies. Remains consist mainly of burials in rock-tombs scattered over the Islands.

The Carthaginians (550-216 B.C.)

The exact period when the Carthaginians took over is not known. What is known is that they supplanted the Phoenicians whose offspring they were. But soon Carthage was no more, and following the Second Punic war Rome became mistress of the world. The Carthaginians left behind them the foundations of the Maltese language.

The Romans (216 B.C.-A.D. 870)

The Roman general Titus Sempronius Gracchus accepted the surrender of the Carthaginian garrison and Malta became part of the Roman Dominions. It was during this period that Malta received her most famous visitor. Saint

HISTORY IN BRIEF – Visitors through the Ages

> "Even St Paul", the Maltese are fond of saying, "even St Paul was shipwrecked in Malta". This is meant to encourage one, but it could also mean that one takes a pessimistic view of anything about to flourish in Malta!

Paul (Paul of Tarsus) was shipwrecked here in A.D. 60 while on his way to Rome to face trial before Caesar. The Apostle stayed in Malta – then known as "Melita" – for three months and converted the islanders to Christianity.

The Acts of the Apostles record that the inhabitants showed them "no small kindness; for kindling a fire they refreshed us all". Greeted by Publius, the "chief man" of the Island, the Apostle cured Publius's father of a fever, and Publius became the first Bishop of Malta.

Commerce and industry flourished under the Romans and Malta became famous for its honey and its cloth. Roman remains are to be found in Mdina, Rabat and at Għajn Tuffieħa.

Honey and Roses

Cicero, the Roman orator and statesman, called Malta "the land of honey and roses". The honey of Malta and Gozo had been known for its excellence and fragrance. It must also have been produced in large quantities. In 70 B.C., when Cicero took part in the impeachment of Verres, a corrupt and greedy Roman Governor of Malta, he demanded of the accused: "I do not ask now where you obtained the four hundred jars of honey …"

The village of Mellieħa was noted for the quality of its honey which was much sought after before the introduction of sugar cane into Europe. It was the Greeks who called the Island 'Melita', which means honey.

There is a Roman apiary in *Imġiebaħ*, near Mellieħa which is worth a visit (*Imġiebaħ* means 'beehives').

The Arabs (A.D. 870-1090)

Imperial Rome fell, and Vandals and Goths ravaged her Empire. It is probable that Roman domination ended around A.D. 454. Little is known about events after that date until the arrival of the Arabs in A.D. 870. The Arabs left few enduring marks apart from a fusion of a kindred idiom into the Punic language of the Islanders. But they did introduce a range of new crops including cotton, and are said to have brought with them the lemon, the orange and the pomegranate.

The Normans (A.D. 1090-1194)

Count Roger of Normandy landed in Malta in July 1090, twenty-four years after his kinsman, William, had conquered England. He was greeted as the "Deliverer of Malta". According to popular tradition, Roger gave the Maltese their national colours – red and white – the colours of the Hauteville family to which he belonged. He also divided the population into Barons, Nobles, Knights, Citizens, Burgesses and Rustics, and thus introduced the feudal system to Malta. The Islands formed part of the Kingdom of Sicily. (A Mass for the repose of the soul of Roger the Norman is still said to this day on each November 4th at the Cathedral in Mdina).

The Spaniards (A.D. 1282-1530)

The Normans were succeeded by the German Emperors of the Swabian House of Hohenstaufen (1194-1266) and by the Angevins (1266-82). The French held on to the Islands for a few months after the Sicilian Vespers, said by some to have been plotted in Malta, had so violently ended their rule in Sicily. They were finally dislodged by Peter I of Aragon, and Malta became the Property of the Spanish throne, held first by the Aragonese (1282-1479) and next by the Castilians (1479-1530).

Several of the great monastic orders settled in Malta during the "Spanish period"; the Franciscans in 1370, the Carmelites (and Benedictine nuns) in 1418, the Augustinians in 1460 and the Dominicans in 1466. The Jesuits came later, in 1592.

King Frederick III visited Malta in 1355 and granted various rights and privileges. It was during this period that the Islands' Municipal Council or *Università*, an elective and aristocratic body, was first established to regulate the internal affairs of the Island. The *Università*, with headquarters in Mdina, played an important part in Maltese affairs, but was no match for the Spanish Kings.

Despite protests, King Alphonse V, heavily in debt, mortgaged the Islands for 30,000 gold florins to a Sicilian Viceroy, Don Antonio Cardona in 1420. When Cardona was succeeded by Don Gonsalvo Monroy the Islanders had had enough. They threw Monroy out and imprisoned his wife, Donna Costanza, in Fort St Angelo. The King threatened to starve the Islanders but peace was restored when the Maltese raised 30,000 florins and redeemed their Island. The King visited Malta in 1430 and promised the Islanders would be "reunited in perpetuity to the Spanish Crown".

The Order of St John (A.D. 1530-1798)

In 1530, Charles V of Aragon broke this promise and gave the Islands to the Order of St John of Jerusalem – the oldest and most famous international order of knighthood. The eight-pointed cross now flies over Grand Harbour.

The Order, whose aristocratic members soon became known as the Knights of Malta, was founded during the time of the First Crusade to help pilgrims visiting the Holy Land. Because of Saracen attacks the "hospitallers" quickly developed into warrior monks, whose prowess was famous in Christendom and feared throughout Islam.

> **The Maltese Falcon**
>
> When giving away Malta to the Order of St John of Jerusalem in 1530, Charles V asked for and received a Maltese falcon which was to be presented to his Viceroy in Sicily on all Saints Day, 1st November. Readers may recall the cinema film with Humphrey Bogart and the sinister Sydney Greenfield, produced in 1941.
>
> Falconry played an important part in imperial courts of the Middle Ages when falcons were trapped and sent to the Monarch who owned the island at the time. Records show that as many as fifty high quality falcons were trapped in one year and transported overseas. The Peregrine Falcon was once a frequent visitor to our shores and was often found at Ta' Ċenċ in Gozo. Unfortunately too many people with too many guns put an end to these welcome visits.

Forced out of the Holy Land, Cyprus and Rhodes, the Order was befriended by the Emperor Charles V, who gave them the Maltese Islands in 1530 "in order that they may perform the duties of their Religion and employ their forces and arms against the perfidious enemies of Holy Faith".

The Order was divided into the following classes: Knights of Justice or Military Knights; Knights of Honour and Devotion; Knights of Magisterial Grace; Chaplains, and Servants-at-Arms or Donats. Before admission the Knights were required to produce proof of nobility on both the father's and the mother's side of eight quaterings.

The Knights of Malta were also divided into eight Langues or Divisions in accordance with the nationality and each Langue had its own Auberge or Inn. The Langues were those of Provence, Auvergne, France, Italy, Aragon, England and Germany. Aragon was later divided making an eighth Langue of Castille and Leon.

The Order's Head was the Grand Master who presided over the Supreme Council. This consisted of the

HISTORY IN BRIEF – Visitors through the Ages

Bishop of the Order, the Heads of each Langue, the Priors, the Conventual Bailiffs and the Knights of the Grand Cross – the senior Knights of the various nationalities.

A remarkable body of religious warriors, who as Gibbons remarked may have "neglected to live", but were "prepared to die" in the service of the Cross.

Soleyman the Magnificent, Sultan of Turkey attacked the Island in 1565 with 40,000 men in what is now known as the Great Siege – one of the most decisive battles in the history of the western world. For four and a half months the Knights and the Maltese, under the leadership of Grand Master La Valette, withstood the fierce onslaught of the Turks. Mustapha Pasha, the Turkish commander-in-chief, swore to take this "cursed rock" and to lead the Grand Master in chains to kneel at the feet of the Sultan. But it was not to be. Malta emerged victorious, and of the original mighty army only about 10,000 returned back to Constantinople to face an enraged Sultan. The victory of 1565, and the more recent victory over the Axis powers in 1943, are celebrated on the 8th September each year.

The Knights were prodigious builders and Valletta, as well as most of the palaces and churches to be found in Malta and Gozo were built during this period. The Grand Master ranked as a ruling prince and the galleys of St John sheltered in the Grand Harbour surrounded by the most powerful fortifications in Europe.

The Maltese Cross

On your sightseeing you are bound to come across the 'Maltese Cross'. This was the badge or logo if you like, chosen by the Knights around the year 1259, and it consists of an eight-pointed cross, which represent the eight beatitudes taught by Christ during the Sermon on the Mount. The four arms of the cross represent the Christian virtues: Prudence, Justice, Temperance and Fortitude.

The French (1789-1800)

The defeat of the Turkish land forces in Malta and later of their fleet at Lepanto ensured the safety of Europe but it also deprived the Order of its *raison d'être*. Decay set in. Many in the Order became tyrannical and dissolute and when Napoleon Bonaparte landed in 1798 hardly a shot was fired in anger. The Knights capitulated and dispersed. Bonaparte has made his intentions clear: he had told The British Ambassador in Paris, "Peace or war depends upon Malta". And so it was. In Malta he set up his quarters in Palazzo Parisio in Valetta (now the Foreign Office) and quickly pillaged the Island in the name of "Equality, Fraternity and Liberty". He left for Egypt after six days leaving behind him a beleaguered garrison under General Vaubois.

On the 2nd September the Maltese rose in open revolt and compelled the French to seek refuge in Valletta. With the help of Nelson's fleet and of British troops the French were ousted and the Maltese asked to be placed under the protection of the British Crown.

The British (A.D. 1800-1964)

Despite Bonaparte's threat to Britain that "peace or war depends on Malta", the Island's accession to the British Empire was confirmed in the Treaty of Paris in 1814. Stable government was reintroduced first under Sir Alexander Ball and later under Governor Maitland, known as "King Tom".

"To visit the Mediterranean" Dr. Johnson once remarked, "is the chief object of all travel". Many agreed with him and several men and women of distinction "discovered" Malta early in the 19th century. Most were captivated by its charm. Coleridge came in 1804 to his "Malta, dear Malta"; Disraeli in 1830; Sir Walter Scott a

HISTORY IN BRIEF – Visitors through the Ages

> **A clerical Major-General**
>
> Since the British Government wished to maintain good relations with the Church, the Bishop of Malta was accorded the privilege of being saluted every time he drove past the Palace Square in Valletta. A standing Order issued by Major-General Pigot, laid down in 1801 that 'His Eminence' the Bishop of Malta is to receive from all guards honour due to a Brigadier-General' (*later amended to Major-General*).

year later to "sniff with great delight the perfume of the oranges" and Edward Lear (of the "Book of Nonsense") in 1848. But Byron viewed it with distaste. His club foot and an unhappy affair with the daughter of an Austrian Baroness did not help. In his "Farewell to Malta" he wrote:

Adieu, ye joys of La Valete!
Adieu, sirocco, sun and sweat!
Adieu, thou Palace rarely entered.

And again, "Adieu, ye cursed streets of stairs – how surely he who mounts you swears!" Not, I am afraid, a very inspired composition.

Anthony Trollope arrived in 1858 to inspect the Post Office (he was a Post Office Surveyor as well as a novelist) and while here he put the finishing touches to his "Dr. Thorne".

On his way to England from Italy, Giuseppe Garibaldi, soldier and patriot, came for two days in 1864 to be cheered by his supporters and booed by his Bourbon opponents.

Malta's great harbour became the headquarters of the British Mediterranean Fleet. The naval dockyard, and income from Service wages became the Island's main source of wealth: the Islands prospered.

Malta played its part in the war of the Crimea when it became known as the "Nurse of the Mediterranean".

> **'From the Halls of Montezuma to the shores of Tripoli'**
>
> An American Naval Squadron cast anchor at Malta in 1801 having arrived in the Mediterranean to try to keep the ruler of Tripoli in order. The Americans decided they would no longer pay 'tribute' in return for immunity for their shipping. After sinking a Tripolitanian ship of 14 guns in the vicinity of Malta the squadron under the command of Edward Preble harassed the Pasha's domain for several years. Unfortunately 'The Philadelphia' was stranded on a reef within range of the Pasha's guns. It was captured and re-floated. Her subsequent destruction by Lieutenant Stephen Decatur in February 1804 was one of the brightest pages in the history of the U.S. navy. It is this incident which is commemorated by the marines song which includes the verse:
>
> *'From the shores of Montezuma*
> *To the shores of Tripoli*
> *We fight our country's battles*
> *On the land and on the Sea'*

Hospital facilities were expanded to accommodate 20,000 patients; in fact some 80,000 passed through.

During the second World War, Malta stood in the front line and the first bombs fell on the Dockyard on the 11th June 1940. Some 30,000 houses were destroyed or damaged during over 3,000 air-raids. The Island stood firm. In a message to Malta, Winston Churchill said: "The eyes of Britain are watching Malta in her struggle day by day" and "we are sure that success as well as glory will reward your efforts".

King George VI awarded the George Cross to Malta in April 1942 "to bear witness to a heroism and devotion to duty that will long be famous in history". President Roosevelt sent a scroll, "to the Island of Malta … alone but unafraid, one tiny flame in the darkness".

HISTORY IN BRIEF – Visitors through the Ages

> **Britain and Malta**
>
> In Valletta's Palace Square on the 'Main Guard' is a Latin description which reads: 'To Great and Unconquered Britain, the love of the Maltese and the voice of Europe confirms these islands. A.D. 1814.
>
> Several members of the British Royal family have visited Malta since then, including: the Queen Mother (as Duchess of York in 1927); Queen Elizabeth II; Prince Philip, Duke of Edinburgh; Prince Charles and Princess Anne. Other visitors were George V, and George VI who awarded the George Cross to Malta; Edward VII and the Dowager Queen Adelaide (widow of George IV).

Churchill and Roosevelt met in Malta in February 1945 on their way to Yalta for their meeting with Stalin. There was some dispute about whether to meet here before, or after Yalta, or whether to meet here at all. Churchill favoured a meeting before and wrote to Roosevelt: "No more let us alter or falter or palter, from Malta to Yalta or Yalta to Malta". When Roosevelt appeared hesitant about the meeting Churchill wrote: "I do

> **War Rations**
>
> A shortage of ammunition, fuel and food created problems for the defenders during World War II. During the height of the protracted siege the civilian ration entitlement for a family of four, for the period 21st to 31st August 1942 was as follows:
>
> Bread: 3/8 of a rotolo per person per day (equal to 300 grams); Corned Beef, 2 tins; Tinned Fish, 2 tins; Rice, Nil; Cheese 3/8 ratal (300 grams); Lard, margarine and/or butter, 1 ratal (800 grams) Edible Oil, Nil; Coffee, ½ ratal (400 grams); Laundry Soap, 2 bars; and Matches, 2 boxes.

not see any other way of realizing our hopes about world organization in five or six days. Even the Almighty took seven. Pray forgive my tenacity".

In September 1964, Malta became an independent sovereign nation within the Commonwealth. In 1974 the Island became a Republic.

An Associate member of the European Union, the island applied for full membership of the EU. This was agreed to early in 2003, and this was confirmed by the electorate in the election held in April 2003.

Today

The island's economy is planned on light industry, the Freeport, the Dockyard and tourism.

This is where you come in.

What to See (1)

Valletta's Streets of Palaces

Valletta is the capital of Malta. With its streets of palaces, magnificent churches and massive fortifications it was described by Sir Walter Scott as "that splendid town, quite like a dream".

Named after Grand Master La Valette who led the Knights of St John and the Maltese to victory over the Turks in 1565, the first stone of the city was laid on March 28th, 1566. All Christendom contributed to its construction: Charles IX of France, Philip II of Spain, Sebastian of Portugal and Pope Pius IV sent gifts and money.

8,000 labourers, including many slaves, toiled for five years to build its two-mile long fortifications about which Samuel Taylor Coleridge wrote: "The fortifications of Valletta are endless. When I first walked about them, I was struck all of a heap with their strangeness, and when I came to understand a little of their purpose, I was overwhelmed with wonder."

There is much beauty here and the places of historic interest are legion. With the help of the plan on pages 44-45 getting around should not prove difficult since Valletta is a well-planned city. Distances are short and once having got to Valletta most visitors will prefer to walk. You can obtain the services of a guide through the "Malta Tourism Authority" in Merchants Street, Valletta (tel. 2291500, Fax 22915893; E-mail info@visitmalta.com; website: www.visitmalta.com);

MALTA and GOZO – Sun, Sea and History

Grand Harbour

1   City Gate Bus Terminus
2   Central Bank
3   Tourist Board Information
4   Air Malta
5   Opera House (site)
6   Museum of Fine Arts
7   Alitalia
8   St. Andrew's Church of Scotland
9   St. Barbara Church
10 St. Francis Church
11 Museum of Archaeology
12 Post Office
13 St. Augustine Church
14 Bank of Valletta
15 Law Courts
16 Manoel Theatre
17 St. Paul's Anglican Cathedral
18 War Relics Museum
19 Italian Cultural Institute
20 Auberge d'Aragon
21 Archbishop Palace
22 HSBC Bank
23 Chamber of Commerce
24 Auberge de Baviere
25 Our Lady of Victory "La Vittoria"
26 Castile Place
27 Upper Barracca Gardens
28 Police Station
29 St. Catherine of Italy Church
30 Auberge de Castile

Plan of Valletta

44

WHAT TO SEE (1) – Valletta's Streets of Palaces

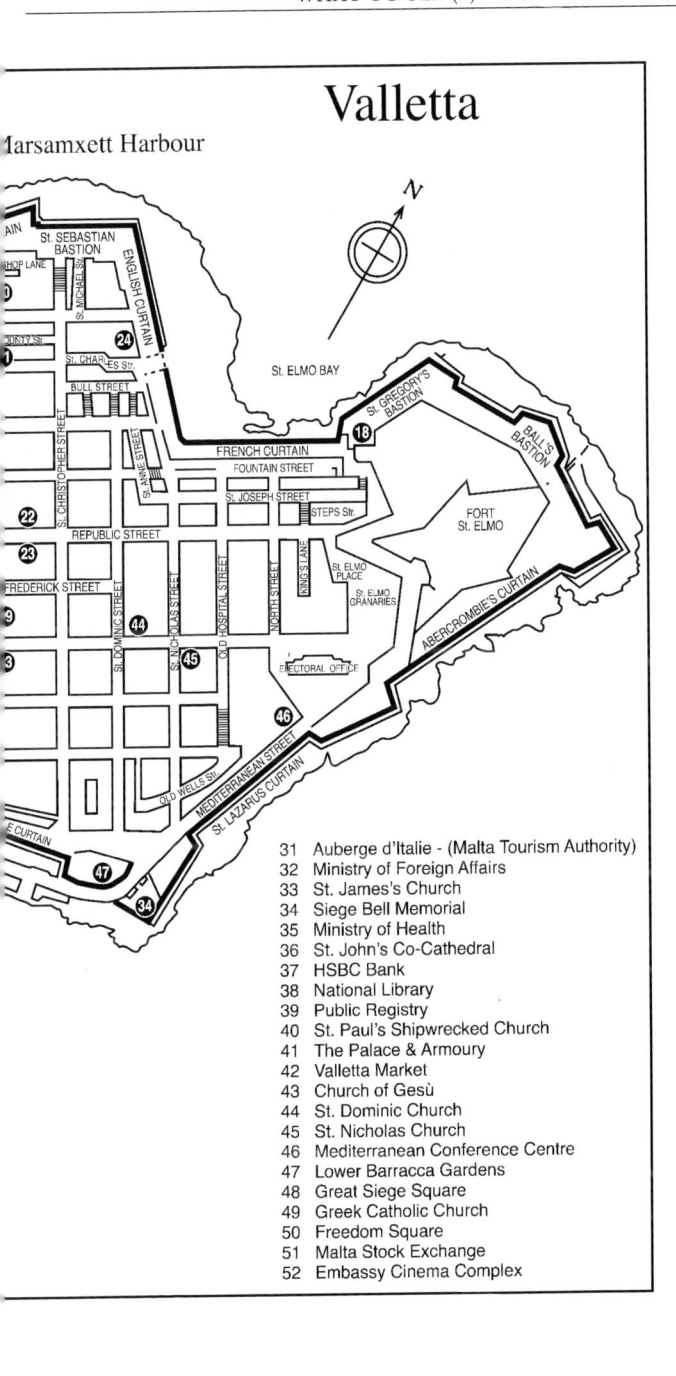

Valletta

31 Auberge d'Italie - (Malta Tourism Authority)
32 Ministry of Foreign Affairs
33 St. James's Church
34 Siege Bell Memorial
35 Ministry of Health
36 St. John's Co-Cathedral
37 HSBC Bank
38 National Library
39 Public Registry
40 St. Paul's Shipwrecked Church
41 The Palace & Armoury
42 Valletta Market
43 Church of Gesù
44 St. Dominic Church
45 St. Nicholas Church
46 Mediterranean Conference Centre
47 Lower Barracca Gardens
48 Great Siege Square
49 Greek Catholic Church
50 Freedom Square
51 Malta Stock Exchange
52 Embassy Cinema Complex

> **Water, water, everywhere
> Not any drop to drink**
>
> One of the problems facing the Order when building Valletta after the Great Siege of 1565 was the lack of water. Initially, water was taken to Valletta from nearby Marsa by barge. A 'city without water is like a corpse' said one inscription. An ambitious project was taken in hand in 1610 and underwater galleys cut in the rock; an aquaduct some nine kilometres long was constructed bringing fresh water from near the village of Dingli. In 1615 water reached the City and a fountain was built in the Palace Square to commemorate the event. An inscription in Latin read: '*Hitherto Valletta was dead. The Spirit of water has now given her life, just as the First Spirit once walked over the waters; now that water has returned to her, the Spirit will return*'. The fountain was erected in the Palace Square to commemorate the event and is now at the Argotti Gardens in Floriana.
>
> The engineer mainly responsible for the Aquaduct was Bontadino de Bontadini from Bologna; unfortunately he got involved in a quarrel and was killed by three Knights.

A Look Around

Before entering Valletta look around you.

With your back to the main gateway (rebuilt in the 1960's) and facing Floriana (the immediate suburb of the capital city) you will see the Hotel Le Meridien Phoenicia to your right. Straight ahead is the Tritons' Fountain (the work of sculptor Vincent Apap) and behind it the monument of Christ the King (by Antonio Sciortino). To the rear and left of the Fountain is the Parish Church of Floriana built in 1771 and dedicated to Publius, the first Bishop of Malta. In front of the Church are the granaries, built by the Knights. Sealed with large stone lids they were in use until recently for conserving stocks of grain.

Also to your left is the eagle-topped monument to the gallant Commonwealth airmen, who died over Malta

WHAT TO SEE (1) – Valletta's Streets of Palaces

during the Second World War and the War Memorial, a tribute to all those who died in the two world wars.

As you enter Valletta through the City Gate (Kingsgate) the first impression is unfavourable for still here are the ruins of the Royal Opera House, which was completely destroyed during World War II (Valletta street map, pages 44-45 – map reference 5). The Opera House was first built in 1861 to a design by Edward Barry, who was responsible for the reconstruction of Covent Garden Theatre in London after the fire of 1865.

Turn left into South Street if you wish to visit the Museum of Fine Arts.

Museum of Fine Arts ✢✢

Enter Valletta through the Main Gate and turn left into South Street. Walk 90 metres or so and the Museum of Fine Arts is on your right. (*Admission fee*). June 16 to September 30: Monday to Saturday 7.45 to 2 p.m.; October 1 to September 30: Monday to Saturday 8.15 to 5 p.m.; Sunday 7.45 to 2 p.m. (*Map reference 6*).

This fine building, formerly known as Admiralty House, was built in 1571. First lived in by Chevalier Jean de Soubiran it was later acquired by the Order of St John and leased to various Knights. Louis de Beaujolais, brother to Louis Philippe, King of France, died here in 1808. In 1821 the palace was leased by the Navy and became the official residence of the British Commander-in-Chief. The Museum opened in 1974.

The first floor houses paintings of the 14th to the 17th century, while the ground floor deals with paintings of the 18th to the 20th century. Rooms 20 to 24 are devoted to works by Maltese artists and the basement is devoted to applied arts, religious relics and Maltese antiques. Works by Tiepolo, Domenico di Michelino, Preti, Favray, Tintoretto and others are permanently displayed here.

National Museum of Archaeology ✧✧

Enter Valletta through the City Gate and walk down Republic Street for about 90 metres. The Museum is on your left. (*Admission fee*). June 16 to September 30, Monday to Saturday 7.45 to 2 p.m.; October 1 to June 15, Monday to Saturday, 8.15 to 2 p.m.; Sunday 8.15 to 4 p.m. (*map reference 11*).

Many art treasures are to be found in Churches, Palaces and private homes but one of the greatest single collections covering Maltese archaeology and history is housed in the National Museum. Formerly one of the Auberges (de Provence) of the Order of St John, this sixteenth century building contains a wide variety of items.

Within the walls of the Museum you can see the remains of the different peoples who have inhabited these Islands: Neolithic, Copper and Bronze ages, through Punic and Roman periods to Medieval times. Among the exhibitions are 'The Maltese Venus' and 'The Sleeping Lady'. The Museum has recently been completely refurbished.

St John's Co-Cathedral and Museum ✧✧✧

The Co-Cathedral and its Museum is situated in St John's Square. Enter Valletta through the City Gate, walk down Republic Street and turn right at the fourth side street (St John's Street). Opening hours: Monday to Friday 9.30 to 12.30 a.m. and 1.30 p.m. to 4.30 p.m., Saturday, 9.30 a.m. to 12.30 p.m. (*Entrance fee except for those attending a service or visiting to pray*.) Sunday for services only.

Thackeray once described the interior of St John's as "magnificent". It is. Designed by the Maltese architect Girolamo Cassar and built in 1573-78, St John's was the Conventual Church of the Order of St John and is typical of the buildings of the late Renaissance.

WHAT TO SEE (1) – Valletta's Streets of Palaces

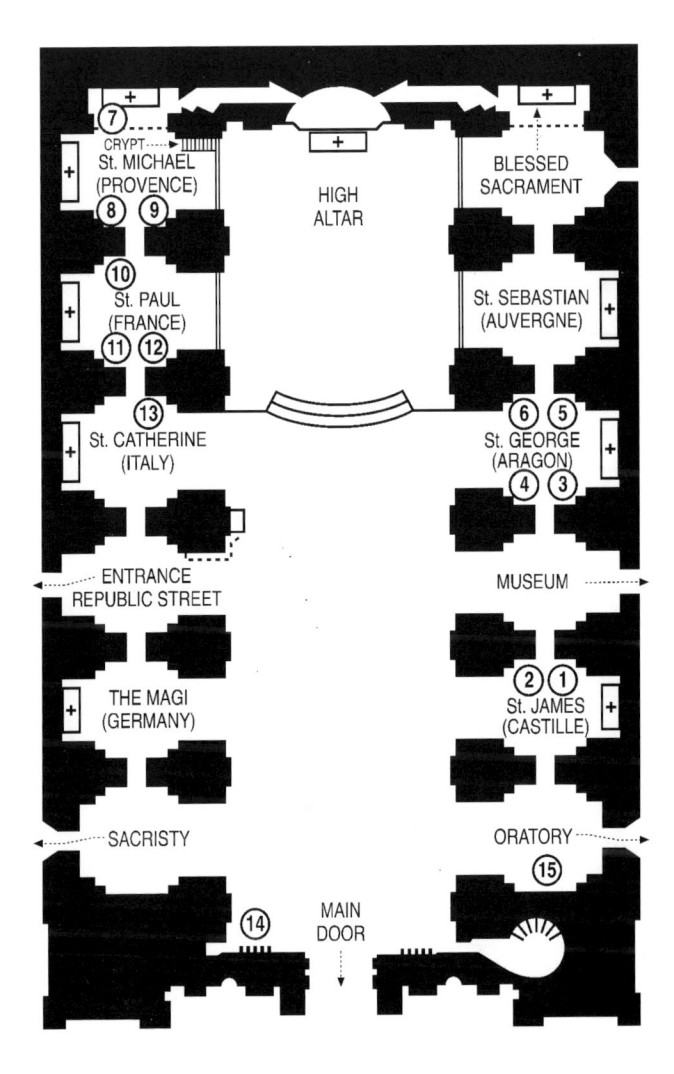

Co-Cathedral of St. John

1. Vilhena
2. Pinto
3. Perellos
4. Rafael Cottoner
5. De Redin
6. Nicolas Cotoner
7. Chapel of Holy Relics
8. De Paule
9. Lascaris
10. Adrian de Wignacourt
11. De Rohan-Poduc
12. Louis-Charles d'Orleans
13. Carafa
14. Zondadari
15. Caravaggio's
    Beheading of St. John

MALTA and GOZO – Sun, Sea and History

St John's Co-Cathedral, Valletta

The Church was built during the reign of Grand Master de Cassiere, and every successive Grand Master took a personal pride in adding to its beauty.

The exterior is austere. The façade is surmounted by the eight-pointed Cross of the Order, underneath which is a bronze bust of the Saviour by Alessandro Algardi (1602-1654). Flanking the front are the two bell towers, and over the portico is the balcony from which the newly elected Grand Master made his first public appearance. The clock has three faces showing the hour, day of the week and month of the year.

The interior of the Co-Cathedral is rich in the extreme. Oblong in shape, it is 57 metres long, 36 metres broad and 19.20 metres high. Eight of the side Chapels belonged to the various nationalities or *Langues* of the Order, and a ninth is known as the Chapel of the Blessed Sacrament and is dedicated to Our Lady of Filermo (*See Plan*, page 49). It is said that the solid silver gates of the Chapel were camouflaged to look like bronze in order to deceive Bonaparte's soldiers. Others disclaim this story and hold that the Cathedral Chapter paid a substantial sum of money to the French to save the gates. Be that as it may, much else was looted including a lamp and chain which was melted down to 172 pieces of solid gold. Treasure was also taken away aboard the French ship of the line, *L'Orient*, which was subsequently sunk by Nelson's guns during the Battle of the Nile.

The tombs of the Grand Masters deserve special attention. Those of Ramon Perellos (1697-1720) and of Nicolas Cotoner (1668-80), both in the Chapel of St George, are superb examples of baroque sculpture. Also buried in St John's is Louis Charles d'Orleans, brother of King Louis-Philippe, who died in Malta in 1808. (*See Plan*).

The paintings on the barrel-vaulted ceiling are by Mattia Preti (1613-1699) and in the Oratory is to be found Caravaggio's masterpiece, "The Beheading of St John". Michelangelo Merisi da Caravaggio (1573-1610) came to Malta in 1608 having been forced to flee from Rome after being involved in a brawl in which a man was killed. His "Beheading" is arguably the most important painting to be found in Malta.

The four hundred memorial slabs "with grinning skeletons and frowning slaves" are in striking mosaic of marble and tell much of the history and valour of the Order which ruled in Malta from 1530 until 1798. One of the Latin inscriptions on these slabs reads: "You who tread on me, you will be trodden upon, reflect on that and pray for me". The position of this slab obliges anyone entering St John's through the Republic Street entrance to tread on it. It commemorates a French Knight, Fra Anselmo de Caijs who, having been passed over when due for promotion,

HIGHLIGHTS – Must Do

St John's Co-Cathedral, Valletta and its Museum
(See Caravaggio's 'Beheading' and the Flemish Tapestries, page 48)

The Manoel Theatre
(Built in 1731 and still in use, see page 59)

The Palace Armoury
(A splendid collection, see page 58)

The Grand Harbour
(A majestic site as seen from the Upper Barrakka Gardens, see page 136)

The Hypogeum at Hal Saflieni
(Awe-inspiring, see page 121)

The ancient capital, **Mdina** (Città Vecchia)
(Unique, visit the Cathedral and the nearby Museum, see pages 89-100)

St Paul's Catacombs, Rabat
(Spooky!, see page 107)

By boat to the island of **Gozo**
(Delightful; visit the Cittadella, the Ġgantija temples and sandy Ramla Bay, see pages 189-205)

By boat to **Comino** island and swim in the **'Blue Lagoon'**
(Ravishing, see page 206)

Take a ride in a horse-drawn **Karozzin** in Valletta, Mdina or Sliema, and in a **Dgħajsa**, a Taxi-boat, from Customs house, Valletta, (*Fun*, see pages 270 and 271).

Visit one of the major military forts
(***St Elmo*** *in Valletta, see pages 65*)

See **'The Malta Experience'**
(History comes alive, see page 70)

Eat **fresh fish** at a sea-side restaurant
(Delicious with chilled white wine, see pages 227–237)

wished to remind the Grand Master that he too would one day be trodden upon.

The Choir is decorated by a striking marble group depicting the baptism of Christ, the work of Giuseppe Mazzuoli (1644-1725) after designs by the Maltese sculptor, Melchior Gafà (1635-1667). The impressive High Altar is of lapis lazuli and other precious stones, and is ascribed to Melchior's brother, Lorenzo Gafà (1630-1710).

In the Crypt of St John's will be found the tomb of Grand Master La Valette. The inscription on his tomb is by Sir Oliver Starkey, La Valette's trusted Secretary, and one of the few English Knights who remained in Malta following the suppression of the English Langue by Henry VIII. The inscription runs: "Here lies Valette, worthy of eternal honour, he who was formerly the terror of Asia and Africa and the shield of Europe, whence by his holy arms he expelled the barbarians, the first to be buried in this beloved city of which he was the founder". (*The Crypt is undergoing restoration and is not normally open except when permission is given by the Curator*).

The Museum of St John ✢✢✢

Opening times for the Museum of St John are: Monday to Friday 9.30 a.m. to 12.30 a.m. and 1.30 p.m. to 4.30 p.m. Saturday 9.30 a.m. to 12.30 p.m. (*Entrance fee*).

A set of magnificent Flemish tapestries are displayed in the Museum next to the Cathedral.

These remarkable works of art were made in Flanders in the seventeenth century after originals by Rubens (1577-1640) and, in the case of the "Last Supper", by Nicholas Poussin (1594-1665). The set consists of fourteen large panels in full colour and fourteen smaller panels *en grisalle*. There is one other panel depicting the donor, Grand Master Perellos.

In 1816, by a decree of Pope Pius VII, St John's was

elevated to the status of Co-Cathedral with equal rights to those enjoyed by the Cathedral of Mdina, the old Capital City.

After leaving St John's and returning to Republic Street you come across the Great Siege Monument on your right. This commemorates the victory of 1565 and is the work of Antonio Sciortino. Opposite the monument are the Courts of Law (*map reference 15*), formerly the site of the Auberge of Auvergne which was destroyed during the Second World War.

National Library of Malta (*Bibliotheca*) ❖

Opening Hours: October 1 to June 15, Monday to Friday 8.15 to 5.45, Saturday 8.15 to 1.15; June 16 to September 30, Monday to Saturday 8.15 to 1.15 p.m. (Tel. 21236585 and 21224338).

In Republic Square, the National Library of Malta, or *Bibliotheca*, built in 1786, contains a fascinating collection of illuminated manuscripts, incunabula and books. Some 10,000 manuscripts covering the twelfth to the nineteenth century and containing the complete archives of the Order of St John are to be found here. The collection includes such priceless works as the fifteenth century "Life of St Anthony Abbott" by Robin Forner of Avignon. There are also numerous letters from the contemporary crowned heads of Europe including the signed bull and letters in which Henry VIII proclaimed himself Head of the Church of England.

Also there are the original bull of Pope Paschal II, dated 1113, instituting the Order of Knights of St John, and the Deed of Donation of Malta and Gozo by Charles V in 1530. In the centre of Republic Square is a statue in white carrera marble of Queen Victoria who reigned from 1837 until 1901. The statue was commissioned on the occasion of the Queen's jubilee and is by Giuseppe Valenti, a talented sculptor from Palermo. Note the Queen's veil made of hand-made Maltese lace (*see page 272*).

Opposite the Library is the seventeenth century Treasury of the Order of St John, now the "Casino Maltese", a Club for gentlemen. The Club has reciprocal arrangements with the Naval & Military Club, The Traveller's Club and the Carlton Club in London. The other Social Club, The Union Club in Tigne (Sliema) also has reciprocal arrangements with various UK Clubs including The National Liberal Club, the Army and Navy Club and the Royal Over-Seas League.

Other Libraries

Other Libraries in Malta include:

The Central Public Library, Floriana. Tel. 21224044.

The University of Malta Library in Msida. Tel. 21320430

The John XXIII Library, 266 St Paul's Street, Valletta (Monday, Wednesday and Friday 4 to 7 p.m. and Saturday 9 a.m. to Noon.)

'The Great Siege'

Next to the National Library you will find a re-enactment of The Great Siege of Malta of 1565, and episodes from the history of the Knights which takes place in the Café Premier Complex in Republic Street, daily from Monday to Sunday – from 9am to last admission at 4pm (*Entrance fee*). Tel. 21247300.

The Palace ✥✥

To visit the State Apartments in the Palace, enter Valletta through the City Gate and walk through Republic Street,

MALTA and GOZO – Sun, Sea and History

The Palace of the Grand Masters

for some 225 metres until you come to the Palace Square. Apartments are normally open to the public from 16 June to 30 September from 8.30 a.m. to 1 p.m., Monday to Friday; and from October 1 to 15 June from 8.30 a.m. to 3.45 p.m., Monday, Tuesday and Wednesday; and from 8.30 a.m. to 4.00 p.m. on Thursday and Friday.

Formerly the abode of the Grand Masters this is now one of the Palaces used by the President of the Republic with the ground floor used as administrative offices. It is with part of the first floor that we are concerned.

Again built to a design by Girolamo Cassar, the

WHAT TO SEE (1) – Valletta's Streets of Palaces

> **"God calls me God"**
>
> The Chapter Hall of the Valletta Palace, became the Hall of St Michael and St George on the institution by Britain of the Order of Chivalry of that name in 1818. The Order was instituted primarily to honour distinguished citizens of Malta. Awards have since deviated widely from that purpose.
>
> The decoration gave rise to a humorous definition:
>
> 'Members rise from C.M.G. (Known in Whitehall, London, as 'Call me God'), to K.C.M.G. ('Kindly Call me God'), to the G.C.M.G. ('God calls me God'!)

Magisterial Palace was completed in 1574 on a site given to the Order by the Inguanez family in return for an annual rent of five grains of wheat and a glass of water from the well in the courtyard.

If you enter through the first Republic Street entrance, you climb up a spacious marble staircase (with low steps specially constructed for gouty Grand Masters and Knights in heavy armour) and find yourself in the Entrance Corridor. This is lined by "Knights" in armour proudly bearing the shield of the various Langues. Numerous sixteenth and seventeenth century paintings adorn the walls of the State Apartments. Among these are the Hall of St Michael and St George (formerly the Supreme Council Chamber). The ceiling is decorated with frescoes painted by Matteo Perez d'Aleccio in 1601 depicting scenes from the Great Siege of 1565. At one end you will see the throne used by the President on State occasions and at the other a wooden gallery said to have been constructed from the poop of one of the galleys of the Order.

Other apartments and corridors full of interest are the Yellow State Room, the Ambassadors' Room, the Prince of Wales Corridor and the Armoury Corridor.

The Tapestry Chamber ✥·✥·✥

Of special interest is the Tapestry Chamber. This is to be found in the Armoury Corridor and was for many years used as the Island's House of Representatives (Parliament). The richly coffered ceiling is very beautiful but the *piece de resistance* is undoubtedly the set of Gobelin Tapestries which are displayed here. Originally designed for Louis XIV of France, these are among the most celebrated of the Gobelin productions. Depicting wild animals and exotic plants each tapestry has the arms of Grand Master Perellos, who purchased them. Some of the tapestries have quite recently been sent to the Mobilier National in Paris for repair. The frieze above the tapestries illustrates naval battles of the Order with the following symbolic figures: Religion, Charity, Virtue, Manhood, Providence, Magnaminity, Naval Victories, Hope and Justice.

There are two main courtyards in one of which you will find a statue of Neptune, (brought there from the fish market by the prudish wife of a former Governor of Malta who felt, one assumes, that it would be less exposed to public view), and in another an interesting clock known as "Pinto's clock" with a number of figures in Turkish costume who punctually strike the hour.

The Armoury ✥·✥·✥

The Palace Armoury contains one of the finest collections of armour in existence. It owes its origin to Grand Master de la Sengle who in, 1551, decided that all arms belonging to the knights were to become the property of the Order. These were to be kept in proper order and to be available in case of need. At one time the Armoury contained enough arms for 25,000 men, and although the number has now been reduced to some 7,000, these include some very early Maximillian as well as French, Milanese, Maltese, English and Saracen specimens. Pikes, helmets, culverins, and cuirasses worn by the Knights, and Turkish guns are all to be found here. The suit of armour worn by Grand Master Adolf de Wignacourt (1601-1622) calls for special attention. Of Italian workmanship it is rich in design and is inlaid with gold. It is ascribed to Geronimo Spacini of Milan.

On the Palace Square, opposite the Palace, is the Chancery of the Order (1602), now housing the Italian Cultural Institute (*map reference 19*). Next door, (the Main Guard), are Offices of the Attorney General. The Latin inscription on top of this building, and below the Royal Arms of Britain, records the start of the British connection.

Casa Rocca Piccola ✣✣

Guided Tours: Monday to Saturday, 10-11 a.m.; 12-1 p.m.; 2-3 p.m. and 4 p.m. (*Entrance fee*).

This 16th century Palazzo is in Republic Street. It is a private family house having beautiful rooms with splendid furniture and paintings and a collection of costumes. (Tel. 21231796).

The Manoel Theatre ✣✣

Guided tours of the Theatre are on held on Monday to Saturday from 10.30 to 11.30. The Theatre Museum is open Monday to Saturday from 10 to 12.30 and from 4 p.m. to 6 p.m. If you enter Valletta through the City Gate, walk down Republic Street and turn left at the sixth street (*map reference 16*). (Tel. 21237396).

This is believed to be the second oldest theatre in Europe still in use, having been built by Grand Master Manoel de Vilhena as a Court Theatre in 1731, "for the honest recreation of the people". On December 4th 1838, Queen Adelaide (widow of William IV) attended a special performance of "Lucia di Lammermoor" and many celebrated plays and operas were performed there. But with the building of the Opera House in Republic Street in 1866 theatrical activities at the Manoel were abandoned. It was converted into a dormitory for beggars who paid 1d. a night for the privilege of sleeping there and was later sold and used as a cinema. In 1955 it reverted to the Government and was renovated. The Theatre is a little gem, with excellent acoustics. Operas, concerts, plays and ballet are held between October and May.

The Auberges

The Auberges, or inns, were the residences of the Knights of different nationalities. It was here that the Knights lived, messed and transacted the business of their respective group. Originally eight in number the Auberges were nearly all designed by the Maltese architect Girolamo Cassar. One, the Auberge d'Allemagne (German Langue) was demolished in 1838 in order to make room for the building of the Anglican Church of St Paul. The Auberge de France in South Street and that of Auvergne in Republic Street were completely destroyed during the War. The following five still stand:

The Auberge de Provence (*map reference 11*) (1571-75) is in Republic Street and now houses the Museum of Archaeology. The Knights of Provence were entrusted with the Defence of the Bastions and Cavalier of St John.

The Auberge de Castille (*map reference 26*) (rebuilt by Grand Master Pinto in 1744) served as Military Headquarters for many years and is the most imposing of the Auberges. It is now the official residence of the Prime Minister. The Knights of Castille and Leon were responsible for the defence of the Bastion of Santa Barbara.

WHAT TO SEE (1) – Valletta's Streets of Palaces

Auberge de Castille

The Auberge d'Italie (*map reference 31*) (1575 and enlarged in 1683), houses the Malta Tourism Authority, opposite the Palazzo Parisio, used as the Foreign Office. The Bastions of St Peter and St Paul were the responsibility of this Langue and the Church of St Catherine was attached to the Auberge.

The Auberge d'Aragon (*map reference 20*) (1571). This fine building is now used by the Ministry of Economic Services. The Knights of this Langue were the defenders of St Andrew's Bastion, and the Church of Our Lady of Pillar belonged to them. It is situated in Independence Square opposite St Paul's Anglican Cathedral. This is the oldest of the seven Auberges built by Girolamo Cassar and is largely preserved in its original state.

The Auberge d'Angleterre and de Baviere (*map reference 24*). (1784). Assigned to the Anglo-Bavarian Knights this Auberge overlooking Marsamxett Harbour, is used by the Housing Authority. (Not far from St Elmo and the War Museum.)

St Paul's Anglican Church ✣✣

Walk down Republic Street until you reach the Palace Square; turn left at Archbishop's Street – in which is situated the Palace of the Archbishop of Malta, (*map reference 21*) – and proceed past Old Bakery Street, Old Mint Street and West Street. Open from 8.30 a.m. to 8 p.m. (*map reference 17*).

Overlooking the entrance to Marsamxett Harbour and situated opposite the Auberge d'Aragon, the Cathedral was built on the site of the Auberge of Germany at the expense of the Dowager Queen Adelaide of England following the recovery of her health in Malta during the winter of 1838-39. The Church is a large, oblong building which combines in a harmonious manner a classic temple and a gothic steeple. The Church was built between 1839 and 1841 by William Scamp. The Church Organ was brought to Malta from the Cathedral in Chester, England.

In the square there is a monument to Dun Mikiel Xerri one of a number of Maltese patriots executed by the French during their occupation in 1798. At the back of the Anglican Cathedral is a plaque commemorating a visit to Malta of Sir Walter Scott in 1831 to what was then the Beverley Hotel.

St Paul Shipwrecked Church ✣✣

Walk down St Paul Street from Castille Place for some 365 metres (*map reference 40*).

WHAT TO SEE (1) – Valletta's Streets of Palaces

Valletta skyline

Built during the reign of Grand Master Alof de Wignacourt (1601-23) at the expense of the Cathedral at Mdina, St Paul Shipwrecked was reconstructed in 1679 by public subscription. It contains many treasures most of which are displayed on the occasion of the Feast of the Saint on the 10th of February. The impressive statue of St Paul which is carried in procession is by Melchior Gafà (1635-67), and the Chapel of the Blessed Sacrament was designed by his brother Lorenzo in 1680. Among the works of art in this Collegiate Church are paintings by Favray, Paladini and Erardi.

'Our Lady of Damascus' ✢✢

Among the ancient icons to be found in Malta, pride of place is often given to 'Our Lady of Damascus', the Byzantine Madonna and Child, venerated at the Greek Catholic Church (*map reference 49*) in Archbishop Street. The Knights of Malta brought this beautiful icon to Malta from Rhodes in 1530. David Talbot Rice of Edinburgh University, and the author of 'Byzantine Art' called the icon 'a thing of great beauty and historic importance in addition to being an expression of faith'. Talbot is inclined to the view that it is even older than the 12th century 'Virgin of Vladimir' now in the Tretyakov Gallery in Moscow. The icon was cleaned at the *Istituto Centrale del Restauro* in Rome between 1963 and 1966 and was freed from the coverage of a Madonna painted in a quite different style that had been superimposed on the original. The restorers were astonished when they finally saw the beautiful Byzantine Madonna and Child, so unlike the previous image.

There is a second ancient icon in the Greek Catholic Church known as the *Eleimonitria* Madonna also brought to Malta from Rhodes. The two icons had been kept safe since 1480 in the church of the Madonna of Damascus

WHAT TO SEE (1) – Valletta's Streets of Palaces

in the city. Originally, the icon was venerated inside an ancient church outside the city walls. The two icons were later transferred to the church of St Demetrius during the Ottoman siege of Rhodes in 1522. The two icons were put on board the Order's carrack and eventually found their way to Malta. The icon was shattered during an air raid in the Second World War and surviving fragments were stored away. After many years of restoration it was formally handed back to the church in Archbishop Street.

Fort St Elmo ✢ ✢ ✢

Walk down the whole length of Republic Street or of Old Bakery Street. Every other Sunday in Summer a live re-enactment takes place of a colourful military parade called *In Guardia*. Guided tours are given after the show – for details pick up a leaflet from the Tourist Office at the City Gate or tel. 21237747.

First built in 1488, and re-built and enlarged in 1533, Fort St Elmo commands a strategic position at the entrance of two harbours – Marsamxett Harbour and Grand Harbour. Its little Chapel, restored in 1649 is dedicated to St Anne. The gallant defenders of St Elmo were massacred after a famous battle during the siege of 1565. The Fort also played an important part during the Second World War and was until recently the Headquarters of the Malta Land Force[1].

---

[1] It is interesting to note that the Royal Malta Artillery, under different title and in various roles, formed part of the British Forces for over 160 years and remained an integral part of the British Regular Army until October 1970.

War Museum ✢ ✢

Housed in Fort St Elmo is the National War Museum. Among the exhibits is "Faith", one of the three Gladiator aircraft – "Hope" and "Charity" were the other two – which made up the total of Malta's air defence at the outbreak of World War II. The Museum is open daily in Summer from 7.45 a.m. to 2 p.m. In Winter it is open Monday to Saturday 8.45 to 5 p.m. and on Sunday from 8.15 a.m. to 4.15 p.m. (*Entrance fee*).

In the North East rampart of Fort St Elmo is the grave of General Sir Ralph Abercromby (1734-1801), a native of Scotland and a distinguished soldier, who defeated the French outside Alexandria in Egypt in 1801 and died of wounds received in battle. In the bastion adjoining Abercromby's Curtain lies buried Vice Admiral Sir Alexander Ball (1757-1808), a personal friend of Lord Nelson and Civil Commissioner of Malta in 1802.

A WALK DOWN MERCHANTS STREET

Merchants Street is one of the busiest thoroughfares in Valletta. It is also one with many fine buildings which are often overlooked.

You get to Merchants Street either from Castille Place, (*map reference 26*), or through the City Gate, veering right at the first turning.

"La Vittoria" ✢

At the top of Merchants Street is St James's Cavalier and the little chapel of Our Lady of Victories – "La Vittoria" – which is the oldest Church in the City (*map reference 25*). Opposite is another Chapel, that of St Catherine (*map reference 29*), adjoining the Auberge d'Italie. The Auberge now used by the Malta Tourism Authority, was built in

WHAT TO SEE (1) – Valletta's Streets of Palaces

Our Lady of Victories Church

1574 and though it has undergone many changes, it still retains much of its beauty and stately simplicity.

Opposite the Auberge is the Ministry of Foreign Affairs, – Palazzo Parisio – (*map reference 32*) where Napoleon in Malta at the head of 38,000 troops set up his Headquarters in June 1798.

As you cross Melita Street, you have St James's Church, built in 1612 enlarged in 1710 and recently restored (*map reference 33*).

Further down on your right is a very lovely building, formerly the *Castellania* and used as the Civil and Criminal Courts by the Order of St John. Built in 1758 it is now used by the Ministry of Health (*map reference 35*). Have a look at the marble statues of Justice and Truth on the façade.

"Il-Monti" ✥

This part of Merchants Street is known as "Il-Monti" and is somewhat similar to London's Petticoat Lane. The market is now located in St James's Ditch, off Castille Place on Sundays. Worth a visit (mornings only).

After crossing St John's Street and St Lucia Street, you come across another handsome building used as the Public Registry, and formerly the Town Hall or Banca Giuratale (*map reference 39*). Opposite, on your right are the Offices of the Consul for Goldsmiths and Silversmiths (who is the appraiser for the Government, and who impresses on Maltese gold and silver his own hallmark).

The Valletta Market, built in 1859-62, and facing the back of the Grand Masters' Palace comes next (*map reference 42*).

Jesuit Church

Further down Merchants Street, after crossing Archbishop Street, you come to the Church of Ġesù built between 1592

WHAT TO SEE (1) – Valletta's Streets of Palaces

and 1600 to a design by Gian Francesco Buonamico (*map reference 43*). This Church is used by the University of Malta (entrance in St Paul's Street) which is the oldest University in the Commonwealth outside Britain.

In 1592, a Jesuit College was founded here. It received the status of a University in 1727 with the Pope's authority to confer the degrees of Master of Philosophy and Doctor of Divinity. In 1769 Grand Master Pinto expelled the Jesuits from Malta (they returned in 1839) and made the University a State University. The University moved to a new site, near Msida, in 1969. This building is now used by the Foundation for International Studies.

After crossing St Christopher Street, you come to the richly decorated Church of St Dominic (1571 but subsequently rebuilt) on your left; and the Church of St Nicholas to your right (*map reference 45*).

Mediterranean Conference Centre ⁘⁘

You are now near Fort St Elmo and if you turn right you will come to the former Hospital of the Order of St John, now used as a Conference Centre. Almost totally destroyed during the Second World War it has been restored to its pristine beauty. Built in 1575 by the Order it did not serve the members of the Order alone but, true to their designation of "Knights Hospitaller" took in the sick and destitute of all races and creeds. The "Great Ward" is believed to be the longest room, unsupported by pillars, in Europe. In its time this hospital or "Sacra Infermeria" was among the foremost in the world.

When the French arrived in 1798 they decreed that the Hospital would be placed at the service of their troops. They melted down much of the silver in order to fund the Egyptian campaign. When the French were ejected by Anglo-Maltese forces, the British turned the *Infermeria* into a Military Hospital.

> **Silver Platters**
>
> Despite their warlike preparations against 'the perfidious enemies of Holy Faith' the Knights did not forget the purpose which had brought them into being. Their hospital known as the 'Sacred Infirmary' became one of the most celebrated institutions of its kind in Europe and enjoyed a high reputation. Built by Grand Master La Cassiere and enlarged by the brothers Cotoner, its great ward is over 400 feet in length and some 35 feet wide, making it one of the longest if not the longest room in Europe. Meals were served off silver plates, much of which was melted down by Napoleon to pay for his troops. The Hospital is now the Mediterranean Conference Centre in Valletta.

'The Malta Experience' ✥✥

Two parts of this building are open to the public. Here one can see *The Malta Experience* with shows every hour Monday to Friday, 11 a.m. to 4 p.m.; Saturday and Sunday 11 a.m. to 1 p.m. (*Entrance fee*). This is an exciting audio-visual show which shows the main events in the history of the Islands using the latest projection techniques.

The other exhibition area is devoted to the *Knights Hospitallers* and consists of a series of tableaux dealing with the work of the Knights. (open Monday to Friday 9.30 a.m. to 4 p.m., Saturday and Sunday 9.30 a.m. to 1 p.m. (*Entrance fee*).

The Siege Bell Memorial ✥

Walking along St Lazarus Bastion, you come next to the Siege Bell Memorial. Dedicated to the men and women who lost their lives during the Second World War and to those who lost their lives in the wartime convoys of 1940-43. The Memorial was unveiled by Queen Elizabeth II and by the President of Malta in 1992. A neo-classical cupola encloses a 12-ton bell, rung each Sunday at noon.

WHAT TO SEE (1) – Valletta's Streets of Palaces

Lascaris War Rooms ✥
Situated in the Lascaris Bastion not far from Customs, the Lascaris War rooms are open Monday to Friday 9.30 a.m. to 4 p.m.; Saturday and Sunday 9.30 a.m. to 12.30 p.m. (*Entrance fee*).

During the Second World War this served as Allied Command Headquarters and operation room of the Royal Air Force and Royal Navy in the Mediterranean.

Sliema and St Julian's

Sliema is the most modern town in Malta, a 20th century residential area with prestigious apartments, and an attractive sea-front. It has long been a holiday resort where standards are usually more polished than found in other areas frequented by visitors.

Even though a shift has taken place during the recent past to the Buġibba-Qawra area, Sliema continues to hold its own as a leading shopping and swimming resort. This is especially true if you add neighbouring St Julian's which boasts of having most of the island's leading hotels and many first-class restaurants. Paceville and St George's Bay provide much entertainment including an Ice Ring, Cinemas, and Nightlife. (see pages 221, 231–233 and 239.)

The De Redin Tower on the Sliema sea front is one of thirteen coastal towers built by the Grand Master of that name between 1658 and 1660.

The Sliema Point Battery better known as 'Il-Fortizza', also on the promenade is Victorian (1876), and is now a restaurant, while Fort Tigne, built in 1792, was the last fortification built by the Order of St John prior to their expulsion from the island by Napoleon. It was this Fort which put up a brave but futile resistance to the invasion by the French in 1798.

St Julian's has Spinola Palace built by a Knight of the Order in 1688 and was used as a military hospital during World War I; also used as a hospital was the Dragonara Palace, built in 1870 by Marquis Scicluna, a Maltese banker.

Buses to Valletta are frequent and you can also get to the capital city by boat from the Strand. (see plan on pages 222 and 223.)

1. The Co-Cathedral of St John, described by William Thackeray, the novelist, as 'magnificent'

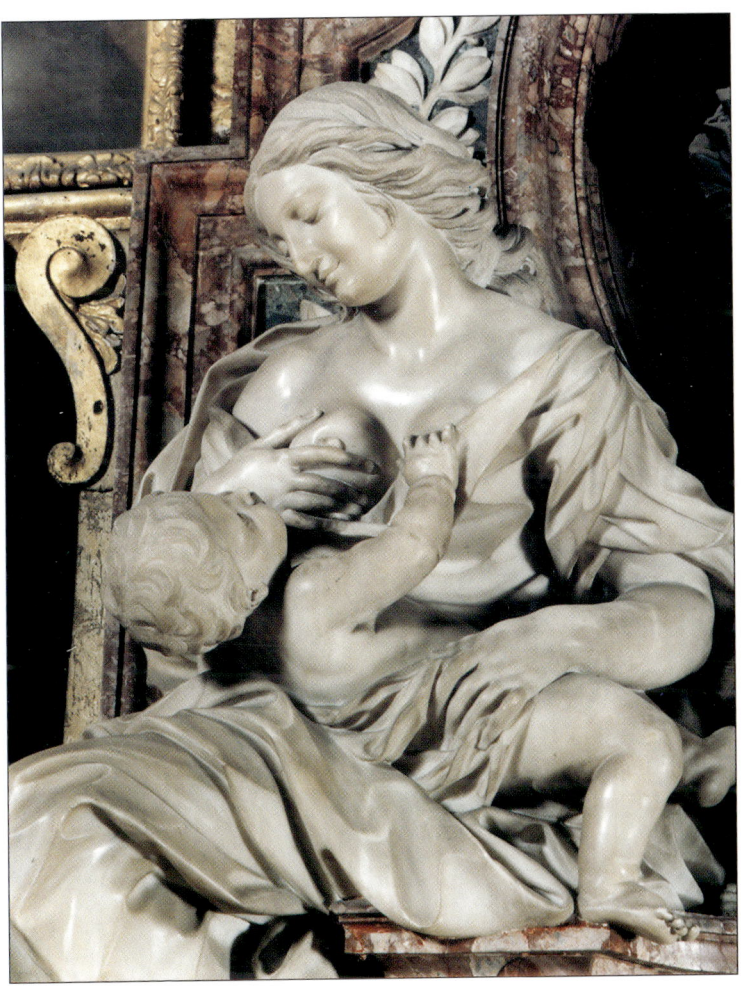

2. A detail of the Madonna and Child from the mausoleum of Ramon Perellos – a splendid Baroque monument in white marble

3. The Grand Harbour from Valletta and (*below*) the Armoury at the Palace

4. The Mediterranean Conference Centre, once the Hospital of the Knights. The great ward is believed to be the longest room unsupported by pillars in Europe

5. A statue in Carrera marble of Queen Victoria (1834-1901), the work of Giuseppe Valenti, to mark the Monarch's Jubilee in 1897

6. The Anglican pro-Cathedral, built at the expense of the Dowager Queen Adelaide of England in 1840, and (*below*) the National Library built in 1786

7. One of the outstanding Gobelin tapestries in the Palace, Valletta – a gift of Grand Master Perellos y Roccaful (1697-1720)

8. The Manoel Theatre built in 1731 and claimed to be the second oldest theatre in Europe still in use

9. A scene from the frescoes depicting the Great Siege of 1565, painted by Matteo Perez d'Aleccio in 1601

10. Ancient icon of Our Lady of Damascus, brought to Malta from Rhodes in 1530 and venerated in the Greek Catholic Church

11. The Museum of Fine Arts in South Street, Valletta and (*below*) one of the sculptures on display – Arab Horses, by Maltese artist Antonio Sciortino (1879-1947)

12. The Palace of the Grand Masters – the main entrance to the Armoury in the 18th century

13. A painting by Antoine Favray (1706-1798) showing Maltese costumes and a Maltese Wall Clock in the background, at the Museum of Fine Arts

14. 'The Adoration of the Magi', one of a set of magnificent Flemish Tapestries woven after paintings by Peter Paul Rubens (1577-1620) at the Museum of St John's Cathedral

15. Senglea from Valletta and (*below*) Fort St Angelo on guard in Grand Harbour

16. The War Memorial in Floriana and (*below*) Queen Victoria surveys the devastation of war – the Palace in Valletta is on the right

Mdina

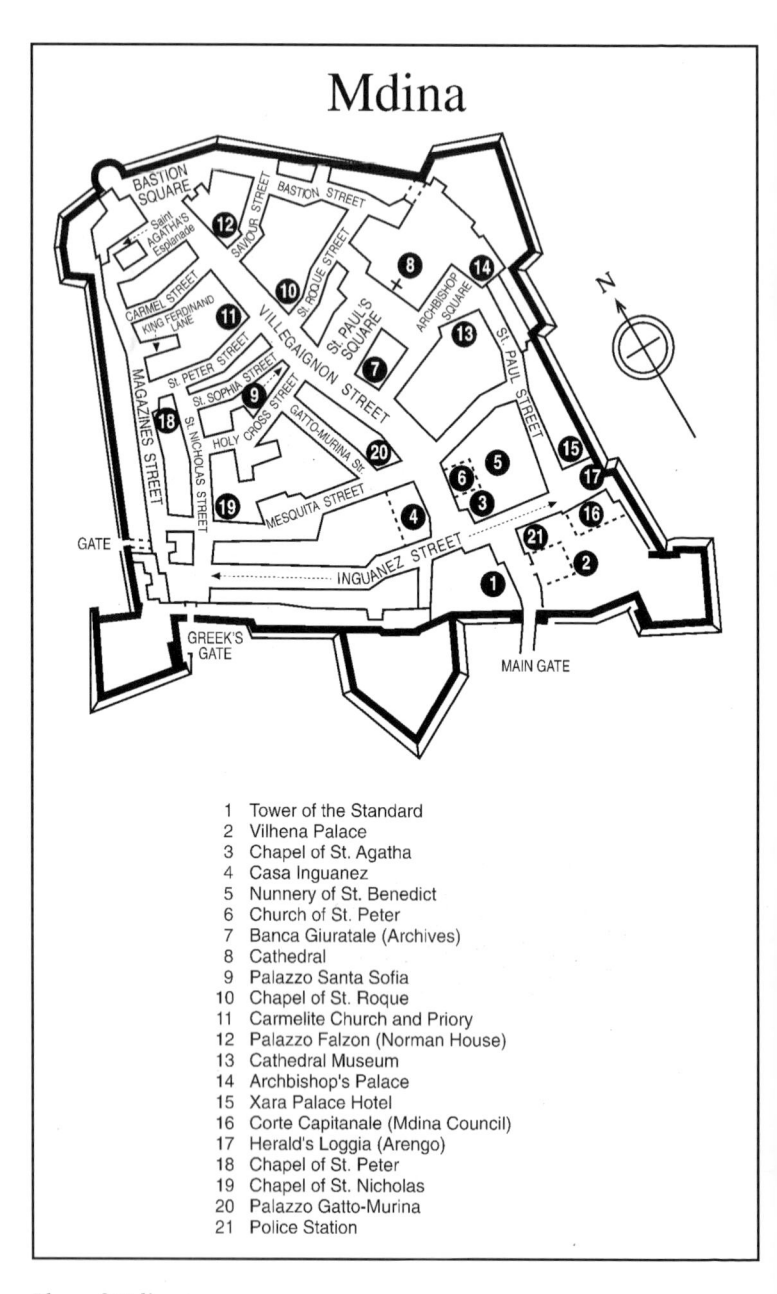

1. Tower of the Standard
2. Vilhena Palace
3. Chapel of St. Agatha
4. Casa Inguanez
5. Nunnery of St. Benedict
6. Church of St. Peter
7. Banca Giuratale (Archives)
8. Cathedral
9. Palazzo Santa Sofia
10. Chapel of St. Roque
11. Carmelite Church and Priory
12. Palazzo Falzon (Norman House)
13. Cathedral Museum
14. Archbishop's Palace
15. Xara Palace Hotel
16. Corte Capitanale (Mdina Council)
17. Herald's Loggia (Arengo)
18. Chapel of St. Peter
19. Chapel of St. Nicholas
20. Palazzo Gatto-Murina
21. Police Station

Plan of Mdina

What to See (2)

Mdina – Proud City

Mdina[1] is the ancient capital of Malta, and its history is as old as the history of the Island. The high plateau on which it is built has been inhabited from prehistoric times. A hill city, proud in its design and aristocratic and ecclesiastical in character, it is one of the few remaining mediaeval and Renaissance towns in existence.

Its earliest known name was Melita, and that was what it was called when St Paul was shipwrecked here in A.D. 60. For reasons of defence the Arabs reduced the Capital City to its present size and changed its name to Medina. In 1428 King Alfonso of Aragon called it Città Notabile. It was the seat of the civil, military and ecclesiastical authorities. Later, when the Knights built Valletta, it was renamed Città Vecchia, the Old City.

Within its walls are to be found churches, monasteries and stately palaces several of which belong to members of the Maltese nobility.[2]

---

[1] Mdina is 12 kilometres away from Valletta. City Gate Terminus Rabat Bus (No. 80). Alight at Rabat (Saqqajja) and walk 45 metres past Howard Gardens to the Main City Gate.

[2] Maltese titles consist of three ranks: Baron, Count and Marquis. The oldest dates back to 1350. No title has been conferred since 1796, and titles of nobility are no longer recognized by the State. Precedence among the nobility is determined not by the degree of the title but by the date of its creation. Some old family names: Inguanez, Sant Cassia, Manduca, De Piro, Testaferrata, Chapelle, Bologna, Preziosi, Castelletti, Stagno and Montalto.

Main Gate, *Città Vecchia*

Several Grand Masters, notably Vilhena, added to the beauty of Città Vecchia and the Spaniard, Martin Garzes, (1595-1601) in an effort to prevent people from moving out of the old city to Valletta decreed that those who lived permanently within its walls should be free from arrest for debt for a period of six years. But relations with the Order were not always warm or cordial,

To walk along its picturesque silent streets is a rewarding experience. Let's stroll along the main thoroughfare – Villegaignon Street – starting from the Main Gate and ending at Bastion Square.

Natural History Museum ✥✥

Enter Mdina through the eighteenth century gate and you are immediately in St Publius "Square". On your left is the Tower of the Standard (*Torre dello Stendardo*) which used to be the City's gatehouse (Mdina street map, page 88 – map reference 1). On your right is the beautiful Municipal Palace built by Grand Master Vilhena (1722-1736) who also strengthened the city's wall and rebuilt its main gate. The Palace designed by the French Military engineer Charles François de Mondion in 1725 is now a Natural History Museum (*map reference 2*). Opening hours as in National Museum (*see page 48*).

Turn left into Villegaignon Street. This street is named after a French Knight who once tried, unsuccessfully, to found a colony in Brazil. Before the last war it was called Strada Reale and before that *"Tal Muyeli"*, which means the street of the gentry.

Palazzo Vilhena, *Città Vecchia*

St Agatha's Chapel ✧⋯✧

The first building of interest is the historic chapel of St Agatha first built in 1410 and re-built in 1694 to a design by Lorenzo Gafà, following the earthquake of 1693 which caused much damage in Mdina. The Chapel which belongs to the Archbishop's Seminary was recently restored and embellished with funds raised by the Mdina Cultural Association. The altarpiece is by Giuseppe D'Arena. St Agatha whose feast day is celebrated on 5th of February sought refugee in Malta in the year 249 after fleeing from persecution in nearby Sicily. The Saint features prominently in Maltese history and together with St Paul and St Publius is one of the three patron saints of Malta. The Saint's image was carried in procession and displayed on the Bastions during an assault by Turkish forces in 1551. The Turks withdrew and attacked the Island of Gozo instead taking many hundred into captivity.

Nunnery of St Benedict ✧ (map reference 5)

On your right is the Nunnery of St Benedict dating back to 1418. The Nuns, belonging as they do to a strict monastic order, are not allowed out of their convent and no man is allowed to enter the building. Even after death the nuns

---

No Entry

The only exception to the rule of 'No Entry' into the Benedictine Convent were the doctor and the white-washer who, in days long gone, and in time of the plague and other dreaded diseases, would apply whitewash which contains lime, to disinfect the walls of the Nunnery. An exception was also made during World War II when a bomb fell on the convent killing two of the nuns.

were, up to 1974 not allowed out: they were buried in a crypt to be found within the Convent. The Monastery Chapel is dedicated to St Peter (*map reference 6*) and its altarpiece, showing the Madonna and child with Saints Benedict, Peter and Scholastica is by Mattia Preti. Prior to 1418 the Monastery was used as a hospital – the Hospital of St Peter – reserved for women patients.

Casa Inguanez

On your left is Casa Inguanez, seat of the doyenne of the Maltese nobility. The Governorship of the Island was almost hereditary in this family until the coming of the Order of St John in 1530. The arms of the Inguanez family are engraved on the inside of the Main Gate together with a bas-relief of the patron saints of the Island. Both King Alfonso V of Aragon in 1432 and King Alfonso XIII of Spain in 1927 were once guests in this Palace. Notice the beautiful door-knockers representing Neptune and his sea horses.

Proceed along Villegaignon Street. On your right is Casa Testaferrata, seat of the Marquis of San Vincenzo Ferreri and on your left Notary Bezzina's House. It is often claimed, erroneously, that it was from a balcony in this house that the Commander of the French Garrison, Citizen Colonel Masson was thrown to his death on 2nd September 1798 after trying to auction tapestries and other valuables belonging to the Carmelite Church. In fact the incident took place in near-by Rabat to which the unfortunate Colonel had gone. Nonetheless when word spread; it marked the beginning of the revolt against the French. This was the signal for the revolt which resulted in Napoleon's expulsion from the Island.

Banca Giuratale

The building on the right at the corner of St Paul's Square is the Banca Giuratale, seat of the Municipal Council, built in 1726, now housing the National Archives (Legal Documents). During the revolt against the French in 1798 the citizens of Mdina formed a National Assembly and appointed representatives to contact Nelson in the fight against Napoleon. The Palazzo Giuratale was used as their headquarters (*map reference 7*).

The Cathedral ✥✥✥ (map reference 8)

You now come to St Paul's Square and face the Metropolitan Cathedral. The Cathedral is said to be built on a site of the house where Publius, "the chief man of the Island" lived, and was converted to Christianity by St Paul.

In the eleventh century it fell on evil times and was restored by Count Roger of Normandy. It was again restored following its destruction by an earthquake in 1693. It is Renaissance in style. The roof of the Cathedral, like that of St John's in Valletta, is superbly painted.

It is probable that a church dedicated to the Blessed Virgin stood on this site from the 4th century. Neglected during rule by the Saracens, it was restored and endowed by Roger de Hauteville soon after his arrival in Malta in 1090. It was enlarged in 1420, the present Cathedral dedicated to St Paul, was built in 1697-1702 after its Siculo-Norman predecessor was partially destroyed in the earthquake of 1693 which devastated parts of Sicily.

Quentin Hughes, sometime Professor of Architecture at the University of Malta wrote: "The Cathedral dominates all other buildings. It is the most important work of the Maltese architect Lorenzo Gafà and is probably the finest domed church on the island ..."

WHAT TO SEE (2) – Mdina – Proud City

The Metropolitan Cathedral, Mdina

The Cathedral has two belfries with six bells, the largest of which was manufactured in 1642: the oldest, christened 'Petronilla' was cast in Venice in 1370.

The Cathedral is in the form of a Latin cross, 52 metres in length and 27 metres wide.

The first chapel as you enter the Cathedral left isle has an altarpiece by Francesco Grandi (1831-1891) depicting the 'Descent of the Holy Spirit'.

The altarpiece in the second chapel represents the Madonna, as protector of Malta by Pietro Gagliardi (1809-1890).

The third bay leads into the Sacristy. The door to the Sacristy, carved in Irish bog oak, stood at the main entrance to the old Cathedral destroyed in 1693.

The third chapel in the left transept is dedicated to 'The Annunciation', a painting by Domenico Bruschi (1840-1910). Also here is a painting by Mattia Preti (1613-1699) depicting St Paul's appearance during the Saracen invasion of 1423.

Next is the Chapel of the Blessed Sacrament, to the left of the chancel. Admire the beautiful silver tabernacle sometimes attributed to Benvenuto Cellini (1500-1571), the Florentine sculptor and goldsmith.

The painting over the altar in the Choir represents the conversion of St Paul and is by Preti.

To the right of the High Altar is the Chapel of the Crucifixion. The striking crucifix carved in wood is by Fra Innocenzo Petralia, a Franciscan.

The altarpiece in the chapel in the right transept is of 'St Publius'. 'The Madonna and St Gaetano' is the altarpiece of the next chapel. Buried here is Lord Strickland of Sizergh, Count della Catena, and Prime Minister of Malta from 1927 to 1932. His daughter Mabel is also buried in the Cathedral.

'St Luke and the Madonna' is the subject of the altarpiece of the last chapel in this aisle.

Cathedral Museum ✣✣✣

Opening Hours: Monday to Friday, 9 a.m. to 4.30 p.m. (last entry 4 p.m.); Saturday 9 a.m. to 1 p.m. (last entry 12.30 p.m.).

The Cathedral Museum was originally a Seminary and was built by Bishop Alpheran de Bussan in 1733. It is well worth a visit.

Despite looting by the French during their short occupation there are many treasures in the Cathedral as well as in the near-by Cathedral Museum, (*map reference 13*). These treasures include twelve large silver figures of the Apostles (now in the Cathedral); an impressive and beautiful collection of engravings by Dürer; a flagon ascribed to the great Benvenuto Cellini (1500-1571); the Cross which Godfrey of Bouillon, leader of the First Crusade, is said to have carried to the Holy Sepulchre the day he captured Jerusalem in 1099; and a painting of the Madonna and Child ascribed by some, wrongfully, to St Luke who was shipwrecked in Malta with St Paul in A.D. 60.

The two brass cannons in front of the Cathedral were brought back to Mdina in 1888 from the Artillery Museum at Woolwich, England.

Returning to Villegaignon Street, the first building on your left is Palazzo Santa Sofia. The first floor was added in 1938 but the ground floor is among the oldest in Mdina and may date back to 1233, (*map reference 9*).

Chapel of St Roque

On the right is the little Chapel of St Roque, which originally stood at the entrance to the City but was demolished and rebuilt in its present position in 1728 (*map reference 10*). St Roque is a Saint whose intercession is much sought after in time of illness.

Our Lady of Mount Carmel ✠ ✠

The next building of importance on the left is the Church and Convent of the Carmelite Order (*map reference 11*). The Carmelite Community first came to Malta in 1370 and established a Convent on the outskirts of Rabat. In 1666 they moved into Notabile. The Altarpiece over the High Altar, 'The Annunciation' is by Stefano Erardi, a Maltese artist active in the 18th century. The painting is said to have been damaged by French troops during their occupation. It was from this Church that the bells were rung to signal the start of the revolt against the French in September 1798.

The 'Norman House'

Further up the road on the right is Palazzo Falzon, commonly known as the 'Norman House', one of the best preserved of the medieval houses in Mdina. It is here that Grand Master L'Isle Adam is said to have taken up residence for a while when he arrived in Malta in 1530. The

---

A Banquet For a Prince

Palazzo Falzon ('The so called Norman House') was where Grand Master Philippe de L'Isle Adam was entertained by members of the Maltese nobility when he arrived in Malta in 1530 and on his first official visit to Mdina, then the Capital. Stonemasons and carpenters renovated the Palazzo. Plenty of wine, crusty bread and sweet honey were purchased, together with two calves and a heifer slaughtered on the occasion of the grand dinner in an attempt to establish close relations with the Order. A gift was presented to the island's new ruler as a token of allegiance, but relations between the Order and the Maltese were not always cordial, and were initially cold.

WHAT TO SEE (2) – Mdina – Proud City

house contains a collection of fine furniture, silver, paintings and books. It is in the process of an extensive refurbishing by the heritage Foundation, *Fondazzjoni Patrimonju Malti* and is to become a state-of-the art Museum.

Bastion Square

Finally, next to Palazzo Falzon we come to Bastion Square and a corner house "Beaulieu", which incorporated part of the Benedictine nunnery of Santa Scolastica, founded in 1496 and used as such until 1604.

The Nunnery was built on the site of a Jewish Synagogue in use in the thirteenth century. Until their expulsion by King Ferdinand and Queen Isabelle of Spain in 1492, the Jews, mainly in commerce and medicine, formed an important part of the Maltese community, and had their own schools, hospitals and cemeteries.

There are many other fine and historically interesting building in Mdina which you can discover for yourself by walking through its narrow, medieval streets with the help of the map on page 88.

Chapel of St Nicholas

If you turn left at Bastion Square down St Agatha's Esplanade you come across several of these, including the Church of St Nicholas first built around 1550 (*map reference 19*); Palazzo Gatto Murina, in Gatto Murina Street, with its fourteenth century façade (*map reference 20*); and finally Greeks Gate (*Porta dei Greci*) one of the three gateways into the City which was built in 1724.

If you turn right at Bastion Square and walk along the city edge you will come back to St Paul's Square and the Cathedral. Near the Cathedral in Archbishop's Square is the Archbishop's Palace, built in 1722. Mdina has always been the seat of the Bishops of Malta who played a leading part in Maltese affairs and often acted as champions of the people and of the city. Also here is the baroque building which was formerly the Archiepiscopal Seminary built in 1733 (*map reference 14*), now used as the Cathedral Museum. Not far from here is the Xara Palace, formerly the seat of the Moscati-Parisio family (now a hotel, *map reference 15*); and in the little piazzetta in front of the hotel, is the *Corte Capitanale*, formerly the Court of Justice (used by the Local Council) and the Loggia from where the town herald read out the latest proclamations (*map reference 17*).

What to See (3)

Rabat and Beyond

After Mdina you might care to explore parts of the suburb of Rabat. If so, you can rest in Howard Gardens, which separate the two, and then walk and look out for the following.

Roman Villa and Museum

From Saqqajja Square (Rabat Bus Terminus) walk through Museum Road on to Museum Esplanade.

Not far from Howard Gardens and next door to the Lower Gate (Greeks Gate) at Mdina, the Roman Villa (Rabat street map, pages 102-103 – *map reference 6*) and Museum is built on the site of a Roman Villa the ruins of which were discovered in 1881. You will find here a comprehensive collection of Roman remains, including a fine marble head of the Emperor Tiberius. The Museum was being refurbished at the time of going to press.

Casa Bernard ✥✥

Casa Bernard at 46 St Paul's Street (not far from the Parish Church), is a 16th century house containing a collection of fine furniture, valuable paintings and other objects d'art. Monday to Saturday 10 a.m.; 11 a.m.; Noon and 1 a.m.

MALTA and GOZO – Sun, Sea and History

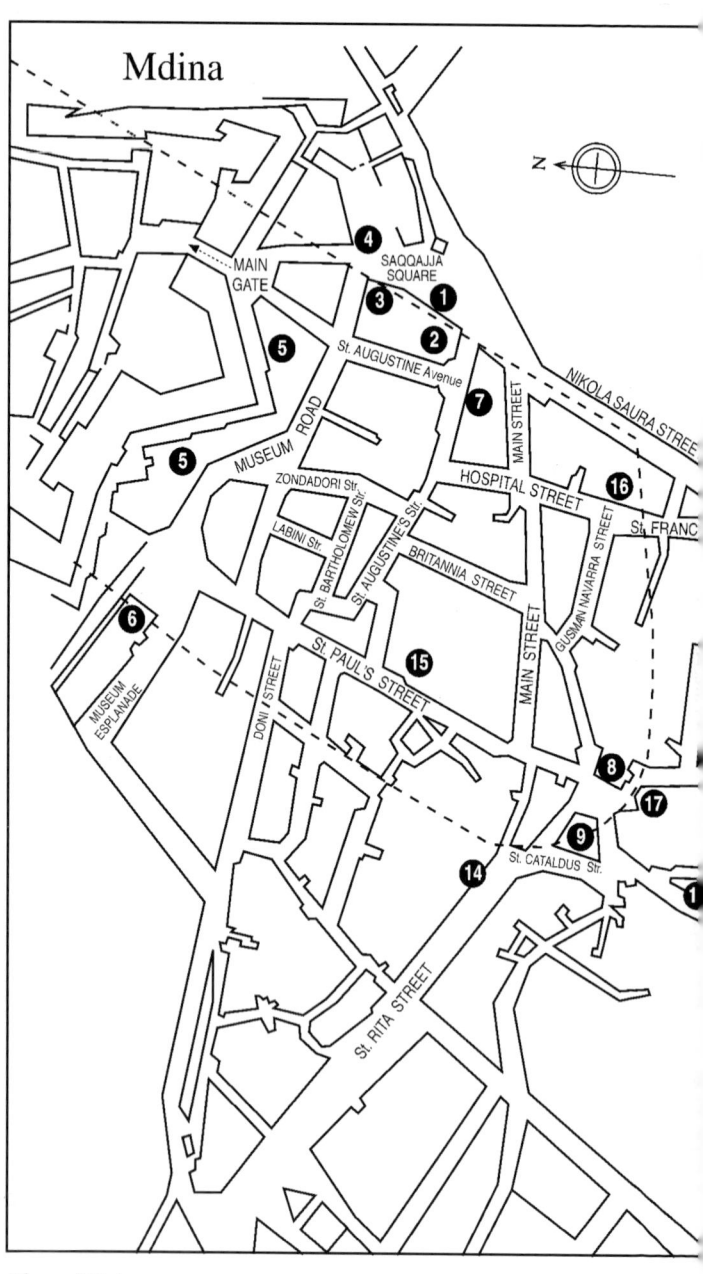

Plan of Rabat

102

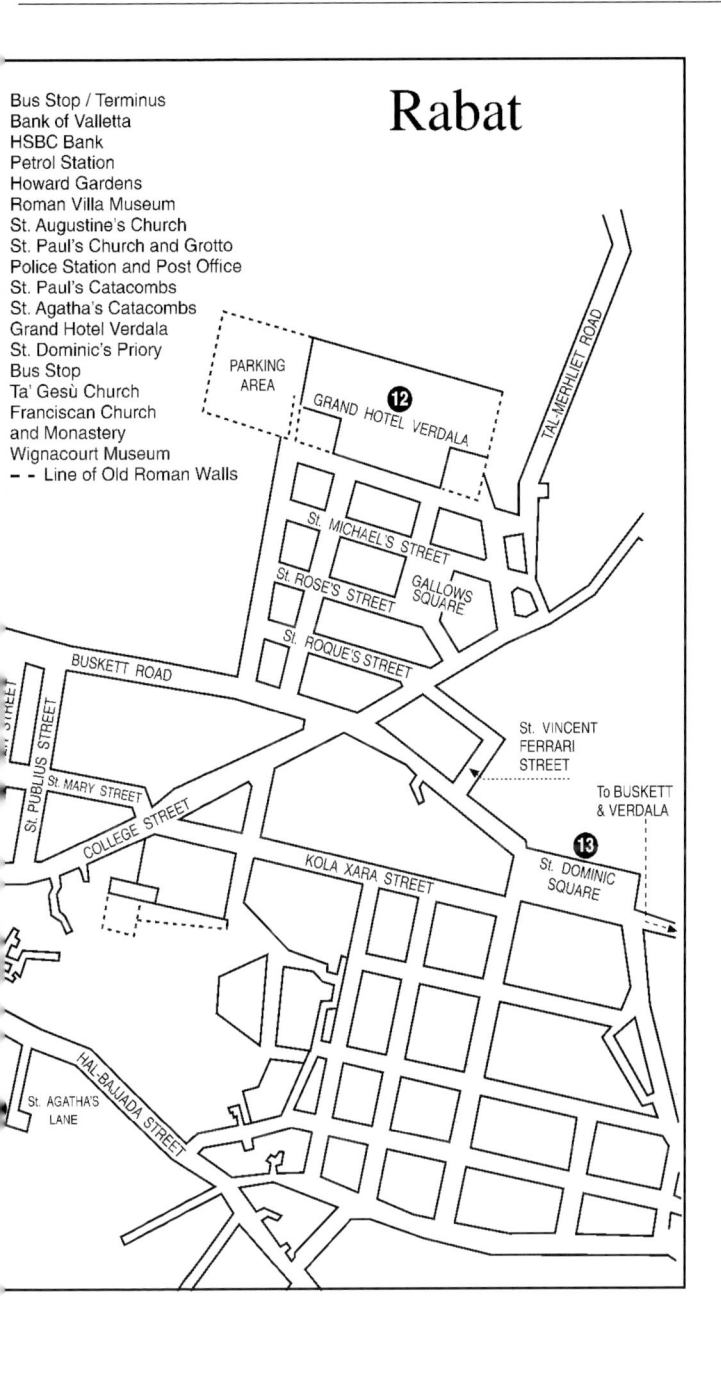

WHAT TO SEE (3) – Rabat and Beyond

Rabat

Bus Stop / Terminus
Bank of Valletta
HSBC Bank
Petrol Station
Howard Gardens
Roman Villa Museum
St. Augustine's Church
St. Paul's Church and Grotto
Police Station and Post Office
St. Paul's Catacombs
St. Agatha's Catacombs
Grand Hotel Verdala
St. Dominic's Priory
Bus Stop
Ta' Gesù Church
Franciscan Church
and Monastery
Wignacourt Museum
-- Line of Old Roman Walls

PARKING AREA

GRAND HOTEL VERDALA ⓬

TAL-MERHLIET ROAD

ST. MICHAEL'S STREET
St. ROSE'S STREET
GALLOWS SQUARE
St. ROQUE'S STREET

BUSKETT ROAD

St. PUBLIUS STREET
St. MARY STREET
COLLEGE STREET

St. VINCENT FERRARI STREET

To BUSKETT & VERDALA

KOLA XARA STREET

St. DOMINIC SQUARE ⓭

HAL-BAJJADA STREET
St. AGATHA'S LANE

Other tours by appointment. *Entrance fee.* (Telephone 21444373).

St Paul's Church and Grotto ✥✥

From Saqqajja Square (Rabat Bus Terminus) follow the road-sign through Main Street, turn left at St Paul's Street and into Parish Square. Open during hours of worship.

Statue of St Paul in the Grotto, Rabat

WHAT TO SEE (3) – Rabat and Beyond

Attached to the Collegiate Church of St Paul in Parish Square is "St Paul's Grotto" (*Rabat map, reference 8*). This is where the Apostle is said to have spent part of his time during his three month stay in Malta following his shipwreck in A.D. 60. The Parish Church was founded in 1575 above a troglodyte chapel which may have been one of the first places of Christian worship on the Island. The Church was damaged during the earthquake of 1693 which destroyed the Cathedral of Mdina. The architect Lorenzo Gafà worked on its restoration and enlargements at the request of Grand Master Lascaris. The large altarpiece of *The Shipwreck of St Paul* is by Stefano Erardi (1683).

Adjoining the Church of St Paul is the chapel of St Publius where the altarpiece is by Mattia Preti. The chapel was built in 1617 by Giovanni Renegues who lived here as a hermit.

From the chapel steps lead down to the Grotto of St Paul which was famous in the 18th century as a place of pilgrimage and was visited by people from all over Europe. Pope Paul II prayed here in 1996, and Admiral Nelson paid a visit in 1800.

Wignacourt College Museum ❖❖ (map reference 17)

An inscription in Latin over the main entrance to the Wignacourt College Museum reads (in translation): 'College of Brother Chaplains of the Order of St John of Jerusalem founded by Grand Master Fra Aloph de Wignacourt on the 1 February 1619'. Several alterations to the building have been carried out over the years, and it is now a fine Baroque Palace with a garden and small chapel. During World War II it was used as a hospital, a centre for refugees and a 'Victory Kitchen' when supplies were running low. There is a large air raid shelter which can be inspected as well as a recently discovered catacomb.

Among the treasures on display are two paintings by

MALTA and GOZO – Sun, Sea and History

Wignacourt Museum, Rabat

WHAT TO SEE (3) – Rabat and Beyond

Mattia Preti, Our Lady of Sorrows and St Peter. A fine portrait by Cassarino of Grand Master Wignacourt, painted in 1617 is prominently displayed. There are many works by Maltese artists including those by Calí, Zahra, Hyzler and Caruana Dingli. Non-Maltese artists contribute a group of five Byzantine icons depicting the Virgin, the Virgin and Child, *Christus Pasus*, the Risen Lord and St Paul holding a scroll. Church vestments, a unique portable altar used on galleys of the Order, an elegant ebony cabinet inlaid with ivory and church organs are among the exhibits.

The Museum is situated next to the Parish Church and is open Monday to Saturday 10 a.m. to 3 p.m. (Entrance fee).

St Paul's Catacombs ✢✢ (map reference 10)

Open Summer 8 a.m. to 2 p.m.; Winter Monday to Saturday 8.15 a.m. to 5 p.m.; Sunday 8.15 a.m. to 4 p.m.; (Entrance fee).

Cross over Parish Square to St Agatha's Street and you find the entrance to the Catacombs. This vast labyrinth of narrow passages, flanked by hundreds of graves, was used as an underground burial place during the fourth and fifth centuries. Vaults belonging to a guild of weavers and to a Jewish family are of special interest. In the former, the tools of a weaver can be seen on the ceiling of the burial chamber and on the latter, the seven-branched candelabrum is carved on the main entrance.

St Agatha's Catacombs ✢✢ (map reference 11)

Walk along St Agatha's Street until you come to St Agatha's Lane. These Catacombs are open for guided tours only: Monday to Saturday 9 a.m. to noon; 1 p.m. to 5 p.m.; Sunday 9 a.m. to noon (Entrance fee).

Though not as large as St Paul's, St Agatha's Catacombs are also of interest especially because of the underground crypt dedicated to the Saint.

Tradition holds that the Saint sought refuge here after fleeing from Catania, Sicily, from persecution by the Emperor Decius in the year 249. According to an old legend, St Agatha, asked by her mother to marry Quintianus, the Prefect of Catania, replied she would do so when she had finished weaving a veil. But like another Penelope, Agatha undid by night what she had woven during the day.

Some important images of Saints dating back to the 12th Century are to be found painted on the walls of the Crypt.

Santo Spirito Hospital

In Hospital Street some 100 metres from the Rabat Bus Terminus is the former Santo Spirito Hospital, now used to house the National Archives.

The Santo Spirito was the first hospital to be established in Malta. It remained the only hospital of any importance until the Knights of St John built their first Infirmary in Vittoriosa, in 1532. The Hospital, whose origin is closely connected with the adjacent Franciscan Convent, was already in existence in 1347. It was closed in 1968, and now houses the National Archives.

In Nikola Saura Street (see plan on pages 102-103) is the Saura Institute, entrusted to the Sisters of Charity and the first private Institution to be devoted to the aged. It was founded on the initiative of a Maltese physician, Dr. Nikol Saura, in 1639.

St Dominic's Priory and Church ✥✥

From Saqqajja Square (Rabat Bus Terminus) walk through Nikol Saura Street and Buskett Road until you reach St Dominic's Square. Admission to the Church is free but permission from the Prior is needed for a visit to the Monastery, although the splendid Cloisters are normally open.

First built in 1466, on the site of the ancient shrine of "Our Lady of the Grotto", it is now a fine baroque church and priory (*map reference 13*) dating from the sixteenth century. During the brief French occupation the Priory was used as a hospital, Bonaparte having decreed that no Religious Order could keep more than one Monastery.

A claim that a figurine of Our Lady of the Grotto had shed tears of blood was being investigated at the time of going to press but already the claim has aroused much interest among the faithful.

There are other fine monasteries in Rabat apart from the Dominican. The Augustinian, in St Augustine Street, has a Church designed by Girolamo Cassar, creator of many of the great buildings of Valletta including St John's Co-Cathedral. The Franciscan monastery in St Francis Street, and that of the Minor Observants in St Paul Street both have interesting baroque churches. (See plan on page 102-103).

Verdala Castle

From St Dominic's Square walk for a kilometre or so through Buskett Road.

Situated on a hilltop overlooking the Buskett Gardens, this Castle was built by Grand Master Cardinal de Verdalle

---

The Blue Lady

The Castle of Verdala was used in 1812 to house 500 French prisoners of war. A chessboard carved in the stone floor of one of the rooms is said to be the work of these soldiers, and this can still be seen. What is more difficult to see is the 'Blue Lady' who is said to roam the castle at night wearing a blue gown. Another Lady is said to haunt parts of St Angelo. Both 'ladies' are friendly. (*see page 170*).

Verdala Castle

in 1588 as his summer residence. Above the entrance to the largest reception hall is his motto "Cedant Curae Loco" – "All cares surrender in this place". Verdala has a Chapel dedicated to St Anthony the Abbott, and the Castle has been adapted for use by the President of Malta, and is not normally open to the public.

Inquisitor's Summer Palace

In a locality known as Girgenti, not far from Verdala Castle, is the Inquisitor's summer Palace built in 1625 by Mgr Visconti on land confiscated from the Falzon family, one of whose members was found guilty of heresy by the Office of the Inquisition! Attached to it, is a chapel dedicated to St Charles Borromeo and built in 1750.

Following restoration, the attractive Palace was placed at the disposal of the Prime Minister. It was kept in readiness for possible use by President Bush of the USA and President Gorbachev of Russia during their Summit held in Malta in December 1989. (For the Inquisitor's Palace in Vittoriosa see page 171).

Buskett Gardens (see page 143)

Dingli Cliffs

Walk past Verdala Castle and follow the road-signs for a mile and a half. Alternatively when you reach St Dominic's Square turn right (towards the village of Dingli) instead of walking straight on to Verdala Castle.

245 metres above sea level with a breath-taking view, the Islet of Filfla can be seen from here. Half a mile in circumference and uninhabited, Filfla was used as a target by ships of the Royal Navy. It is now a Nature Reserve.

Medieval Hamlet

West of Dingli are the remains of a medieval hamlet known as *Is-simblija* consisting of a Medieval chapel, a bakery and a kitchen. Energetic hitch-hikers can make their way to the 'Bobbyland Restaurant' and follow the signs.

17. Aerial view of the old Capital City and (*below*) a 19th century painting of Mdina by the Schranz Brothers

18. The Metropolitan Cathedral in Mdina

19. The Arms of Grand Master Vilhena on the façade and (*below*) the patron Saints of Mdina – St Publius, St Paul and St Agatha – on the inside of the entrance to the City

20. The Tower of the Standard at the entrance to the city

21. The Main Gate to Mdina and (*below*) Città Vecchia by night

22. Sunset over the 'City of all Time'

23. Parish Church of St Paul in Rabat

24. The splendid cloister at St Dominic's Priory and (*below*) The Catacombs in Rabat

25. Palazzo Vilhena by night

120

What to See (4)

Prehistoric Sites and Temples

Malta is rich in places of archaeological interest, and there are probably more unique prehistoric sites and temples to the square mile than anywhere else in the world. Colin Renfrew in his *Before Civilization* (1973) wrote: 'The great temples of Malta lay claim to be the world's most impressive prehistoric monuments ... according to radiocarbon chronology, the temples are the earliest free-standing monuments of stone in the world'. This makes them older than the pyramids of Egypt, and of Stonehenge in England. These temples were constructed and decorated in a manner befitting the gods. Not for nothing was Malta once venerated as the "Sacred Island of the Mediterranean".

Here are some of the better known sites:

The Hypogeum (*Hal Saflieni*)[1] ✣✣✣

Cospicua bus (No.1) from City Gate Terminus. Alight at Paola Square, walk straight on for about 183 metres; turn to your right from Luqa Road corner with Burials Street.

This elaborately decorated underground temple

---

[1] Opening hours for state-owned Museums are: October 1 to June 15, 8.15 a.m. to 5 p.m. (Sunday 4.15); and June 16 to September 30: 7.45 a.m. to 2 p.m.

MALTA and GOZO – Sun, Sea and History

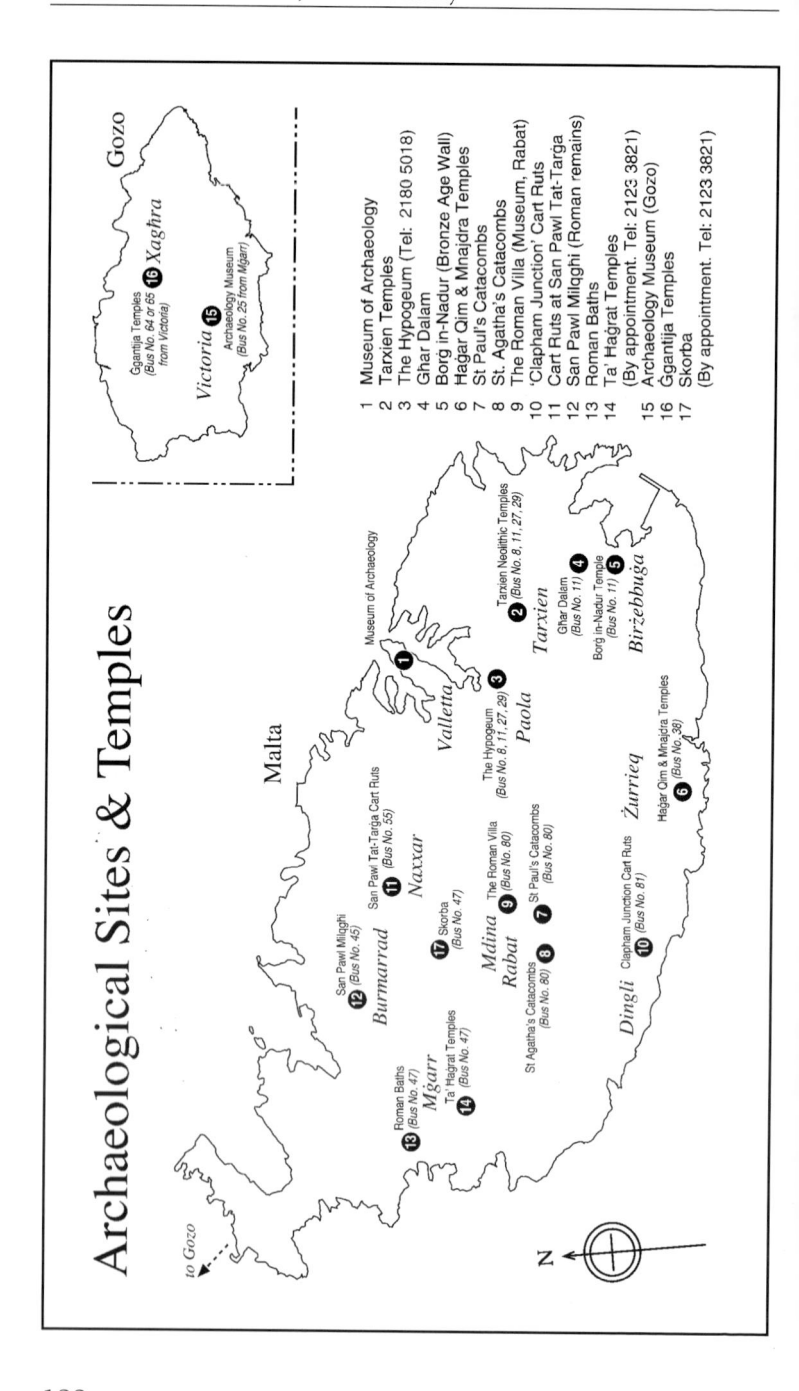

Archaeological Sites & Temples

1. Museum of Archaeology
2. Tarxien Temples
3. The Hypogeum (Tel: 2180 5018)
4. Ghar Dalam
5. Borg in-Nadur (Bronze Age Wall)
6. Ħaġar Qim & Mnajdra Temples
7. St Paul's Catacombs
8. St. Agatha's Catacombs
9. The Roman Villa (Museum, Rabat)
10. 'Clapham Junction' Cart Ruts
11. Cart Ruts at San Pawl Tat-Targa
12. San Pawl Milqghi (Roman remains)
13. Roman Baths
14. Ta' Ħagrat Temples
    (By appointment. Tel: 2123 3821)
15. Archaeology Museum (Gozo)
16. Ggantija Temples
17. Skorba
    (By appointment. Tel: 2123 3821)

122

(c. 2500 B.C.) hallowed out of the solid rock, should be counted among the wonders of the world. The construction of this monument must have taken ages to complete and the people who planned it must have reached a high degree of civilization. Of special interest is the Holy of Holies and the Oracle Chamber where a murmur, properly directed, becomes magnified many times and booms throughout the temple (Archaeological Sites and Temples, page 122, *reference 3*).

Some authorities hold that the Hypogeum was a sanctuary where devotees were able to consult an oracle under the direction of a priesthood who, among other things, interpreted dreams, during sleep which may have been induced by drugs or hypnotism. The Hypogeum is a UNESCO World Heritage Site. Not more than ten persons are allowed in at any one time. (Telephone 21805018) (*Entrance fee*)

Tarxien Temples and Museum ❖❖❖ (map reference 2)

Żejtun (No. 26) or Kalafrana (No. 12) bus from City Gate Terminus. Ask the conductor to put you down near the Tarxien Police Station; walk some 18 metres and turn left at the first corner.

A group of four Neolithic temples discovered by accident in 1913. As in the case of the Hypogeum there is a great deal of value to the visitor interested in prehistoric culture in the Mediterranean. The temples were converted into cremation cemeteries during the Bronze Age (c. 2400 B.C.). (Telephone 21695578)

Ħaġar Qim and Mnajdra Temples ❖❖❖

Żurrieq (No. 32) bus from City Gate Terminus. Alight at Qrendi Terminus and follow road signs for about a kilometre. Admission fee. Open every day. (Telephone 21221623)

Excavated in 1840 and 1893, these two groups of megalithic temples (2800 B.C.) stand some 365 metres apart and are among the best preserved on the Island. Ħaġar Qim (*map reference 6*) is best known for the statuettes of "fat divinities", characteristic of Stone Age worship in

The temple at Ħaġar Qim

Malta, which were found here. Notice the huge stone near the north-east wall measuring 7 metres by 2.74 metres. As you walk towards Mnajdra you can see the Island of Filfla to your left.

Għar Dalam ✥✥✥ (map reference 4)

Kalafrana (No. 12) bus from City Gate Terminus. Ask the conductor to put you down at last bus stop before arriving at St George's Bay, Birżebbugia. (Telephone 21675419)

Literally the "cave of darkness" where many fossil remains of animals which roamed the Island in 3800 B.C. were found. These include remains of the dwarf hippopotami, elephants, wolf, bear, stag and giant tortoise, and are to be seen in the Museum built over the large cave. Anthropologists still argue over two molar teeth discovered in 1917 and attributed by some to Neanderthal man.

Cart-Ruts ✥✥

The prehistoric "cart-ruts" which exist in large numbers and are widely scattered over the Island have long puzzled archaeologists. The tracks consist of parallel grooves some 25 to 50 cm wide at the surface level, around 137 cm apart and between 5 cm and 60 cm deep. Whether these tracks were cut by the wheels of heavy carts, or shafts, or by human labour, has never been clearly determined. The purpose for which they were used and what exactly was transported along these "tram-lines" also remains a mystery.

The late Sir Themistocles Zammit the celebrated Maltese physician and archaeologist wrote: "They tell a story of immense activity on the part of a considerable population engaged in the transport of a heavy material on hundreds of carts and for hundreds of years".

PREHISTORIC CULTURAL SEQUENCE

Period	Phase	Approx. Date	Landscape features visible today
Neolithic	Għar Dalam Grey Skorba Red Skorba	5200-4500 BC. 4500-4400 BC. 4400-4100 BC.	Remnants of villages
Copper Age	Żebbuġ Mġarr Ġgantija Saflieni Tarxien	4100-3800 BC. 3800-3600 BC. 3600-3000 BC. 3300-3000 BC. 3000-2500 BC.	Rock-cut tombs Rock-cut tombs; numerous temples Tarxien temples
Bronze Age	Tarxien Cemetry Borg in-Nadur Bahrija	2500-1500 BC. 900-8th Century BC.	Cremation cemetery, and dolmens Fortified villages Fortified villages

WHAT TO SEE (4) – Prehistoric Sites and Temples

The ancient cart-tracks are found in many areas including Mtarfa, Wardija, Bingemma (near Nadur Tower), San Pawl tat-Targa (*map reference 11*), and to the south of Verdala Castle near the Inquisitors Palace at Girgenti, (known as 'Clapham Junction'), and near the signal station at Dingli.

Ġgantija Temples ❖❖❖ (see page 196)

Prehistoric Cultural Sequence (see page 126)

(See plan of archaeological sites; page 122, with the buses which will get you there.)

MALTA and GOZO – Sun, Sea and History

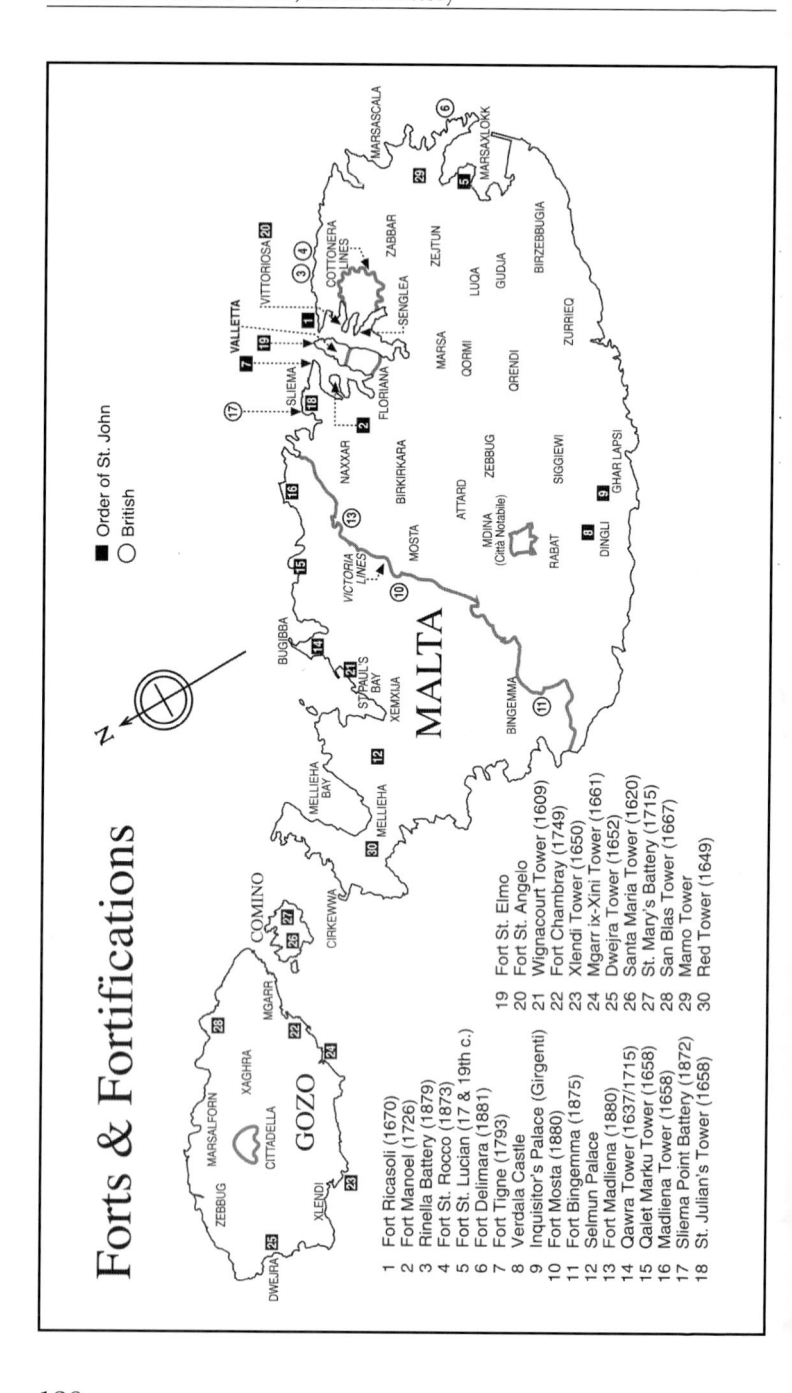

Forts & Fortifications

- Order of St. John
- British

1 Fort Ricasoli (1670)
2 Fort Manoel (1726)
3 Rinella Battery (1879)
4 Fort St. Rocco (1873)
5 Fort St. Lucian (17 & 19th c.)
6 Fort Delimara (1881)
7 Fort Tigne (1793)
8 Verdala Castle
9 Inquisitor's Palace (Girgenti)
10 Fort Mosta (1880)
11 Fort Bingemma (1875)
12 Selmun Palace
13 Fort Madliena (1880)
14 Qawra Tower (1637/1715)
15 Qalet Marku Tower (1658)
16 Madliena Tower (1658)
17 Sliema Point Battery (1872)
18 St. Julian's Tower (1658)
19 Fort St. Elmo
20 Fort St. Angelo
21 Wignacourt Tower (1609)
22 Fort Chambray (1749)
23 Xlendi Tower (1650)
24 Mgarr ix-Xini Tower (1661)
25 Dwejra Tower (1652)
26 Santa Maria Tower (1620)
27 St. Mary's Battery (1715)
28 San Blas Tower (1667)
29 Mamo Tower
30 Red Tower (1649)

128

What to See (5)

Forts and Fortifications

The Knights and the British

The fortifications of Malta are massive. The Knights of the Order of St John having been expelled from the Holy Land and from Rhodes were determined not to have history repeat itself.

During a visit to Malta in 1834, Samuel Taylor Coleridge, was impressed by the fortifications, which he called 'bulky breasted heights', and he wrote that the fortifications 'are endless. When I first walked about them, I was struck all of a heap with their strangeness, and when I came to understand a little of their purpose, I was overwhelmed with wonder".

Quentin Hughes, sometime Professor of Architecture at the University of Malta, in his book *Fortress* wrote: 'From time immemorial, the Maltese islands have been the scene of monumental building'. Lying strategically in the centre of the Mediterranean the best defence against invaders was 'afforded by the build-up of long lines of defence and an intricate system of fortification. Look-out towers gave warning, forts guarded the bays and creeks, castles gave some measure of protection to the wealthy who dwelt in the countryside, and miles of outworks, bastion, cavaliers, and curtain walls were spun around the main centres of population. This has resulted in one of the most complex *enceintes* in the history of military architecture.'

Senglea

Miles and miles of massive walls enclose Valletta and Floriana, Mdina and the three cities of Vittoriosa, Senglea and Cospicua, and the Cittadella in Gozo.

The Knights were determined to make Malta impregnable. To strengthen the defence of the Three Cities the Order invited Vincenzo Masculano da Firenzuola, a prominent Italian engineer who designed the Margherita

WHAT TO SEE (5) – Forts and Fortifications

Lines. Grand Master Nicolas Cotoner wanted something even more grandiose and he commissioned another Italian engineer to come to Malta in 1663. The result was the monumental line of fortifications which sealed off Vittoriosa, Cospicua and Senglea from a landward attacks, and in a desire to perpetuate his name and fame the fortifications were known as the Cottonera Lines. (*See Plan, page 184.*) For those sufficiently energetic who wish to view these wonderful fortifications, St Helen's Gate in Cospicua, and Salvatore Gate on the outskirts of Vittoriosa are good starting points. (See Plan on pages 168-169.)

The Grand Harbour is dominated by the huge forts of Ricasoli, (1670), St Angelo (a fort has existed here since ancient time), and St Elmo which stands on the site of a small tower built before 1481. The Fort guards the approaches of both Grand Harbour and Marsamxett Harbour. *Open on Saturday from 1 p.m. to 5 p.m. and on Sundays from 9 a.m. to 5 p.m. Tours start fifteen minutes past the hour (Entrance fee).*

St Angelo, Vittoriosa is open from 10 a.m. until 2 p.m. on Saturday; from 1st June to 30 September from 9 a.m. to 1 p.m. Tours start at 15 minutes past the hour (Entrance fee).

Other Forts of interest include Fort Manoel on Manoel Island built in 1723, and now being resotred.

Wignacourt Tower (1609) in St Paul's Bay – this is open from 9.30 a.m. to 12 noon. Monday to Friday. Entrance is free, though donations to *Din l-Art Ħelwa* which helped to restore it are welcome. Wignacourt is the oldest surviving coastal tower in Malta.

Wignacourt Tower, St Paul's Bay

The Red Tower, Mellieha

WHAT TO SEE (5) – Forts and Fortifications

De Redin coastal tower

St Agatha's Tower, also known as the Red Tower, in Mellieħa, built in 1647 by Grand Master Lascaris, a Frenchman, is likewise open from 9.30 a.m. to 12.40 p.m. daily.

Between 1658 and 1660 a string of thirteen coastal towers were built by Grand Master de Redin, a Spaniard, and of these eight still stand (See plan, page 128).

British Fortifications

The British added to the fortifications. They improved the defence of the Islands' harbours and strengthened the defences of the southwest coast with the addition of Forts Leonardo, San Lucian and Bengħajsa.

They also built the so-called Victoria Lines a series of fortifications some 12 kilometres in length, which cut across the island from Fomm ir-Riħ Bay in the West to Madliena in the East. Forts Binġemma, Mosta and Madliena were built first to be followed by Fort Pembroke. The 'Lines' were built between 1870 and 1899 and were given their present name in 1897 in commemoration of Queen Victoria's Diamond Jubilee.

The Victoria Lines were never tested in time of war and were abandoned soon after The Great War. They fell into disrepair but efforts are now being made to restore them and several walks are to be had here. Probably the easiest place to get to the Victoria Lines by bus is to go to Targa Gap – not far from Mosta.

Fort Mosta (1878) is open for visits from 9.30 a.m. to 12.30 p.m. daily: tours at 9.30, 10.30 and 11.30 a.m.

Fort Madliena also built in 1878, is open from 10 a.m. to 1 p.m. on a Sunday: Guided Tours at 10, 11 and 12 noon.

Other Forts built by the British include San Rocco and San Leonardo and Fort Binġemma none of which are open to the public.

Fort Rinella

Fort Rinella (1878) in St Rocco Road, Kalkara, houses the world largest cannon – a British muzzle-loading 100 ton gun built to a design by Sir William Armstrong around 1880. A re-enactment takes place every Saturday afternoon between 2 and 4.30 p.m.

WHAT TO SEE (5) – Forts and Fortifications

> Malta's connection with the Royal Navy dates back to 1674 when King Charles II wrote to 'our cousin and friend', Grand Master Cotoner, informing him that Barbary pirates had obliged him to keep a squadron permanently in the Mediterranean and asking 'the most eminent Prince' for facilities to purchase slave crews and provisions. In August 1675 a squadron under Admiral Sir John Narborough called at Malta.

Opening Hours: 1ˢᵗ October to mid-June, Monday to Saturday 10 a.m. to 4 p.m.; Sunday 1 p.m. to 4 p.m. Mid-June to September 9.30 a.m. to 1 p.m.; Sunday 10 a.m. to 1 p.m. Closed on Public Holidays (Entrance fee). (Bus No 4 from Valletta to Kalkara at the Rinella Movie Park and then follow the sign posts. The Fort is being renovated by 'Fondazzjoni Wirt Artna', a Heritage Foundation. (Telephone 31580688)

In Gozo

Impressive fortifications in Gozo include the Citadel (*Victoria, Bus 25 from Mġarr*) and Fort Chambray (1757), which is being developed into a Tourist Complex (*Bus 25 from Mġarr*).

What to See (6)

Gardens and Garden Centres

> *"God Almighty first planted a garden,
> and indeed it is the purest of human pleasures"*
> (Francis Bacon)

IN VALLETTA

Sightseeing can be tiring and every now and then you will want to sit and rest. What better place than a public garden? There are three in Valletta, the best known of which is the Upper Baracca.

Upper Baracca ✣✣✣ (Valletta map, reference 27)

Enter Valletta through Castille Square and walk about 18 metres to your right.

Not far from the Auberge de Castille, this delightful spot on a lofty part of the fortifications commands a magnificent view of the Grand Harbour, at the entrance of which stands Fort Ricasoli.

Several memorials are to be found in these as well as in other ramparts and some are unusual in that they surmount the grave of the person commemorated. One author wrote in 1839: "Since the British became masters in

Malta, the proud bastions of Valletta have become sepulchral".

Among the memorials at the Upper Barrakka are those to Vice-Admiral Sir Thomas Fremantle (1765-1819) a close associate of Nelson. The Australian port of Fremantle is named after his cousin, Admiral Sir Charles Fremantle, and his grandnephew, General Sir Arthur Fremantle, was Governor of Malta in 1893-99.

Also here is a memorial to Sir Thomas Maitland, Governor of Malta from 1813 to 1824; and to Lord Strickland, Count della Catena, one-time Governor of New South Wales and Western Australia and Prime Minister of Malta from 1927 to 1932.

In the left-hand corner of the gardens is *Les Gavroches*, a group suggested by an incident in Victor Hugo's *Les Miserables*. It is one of the first important works of the distinguished Maltese sculptor Antonio Sciortino. In 1951, the sculptor's small bronze model was presented to Queen Elizabeth by the Prime Minister of Malta.

The latest addition to the monuments of the Upper Barrakka[1] is a bronze bust of Winston Churchill (the work of Vincent Apap) presented to Sir Winston in 1955 by the people of Malta.

The Upper Barracca dates back to 1661 when part of the garden was covered. The roof, it is said, was removed in 1755 when it was discovered that the spot had been used by conspirators involved in what has become known as the "Revolt of the Priests". This aimed at the overthrow of Grand Master Ximenes and was led by one Don Gaetano Mannarino, who was subsequently imprisoned for life but released by Napoleon in 1798.

---

[1] The Upper Barracca is the setting of an episode in the novel "Grand Harbour" by Bradda Field (Constable, 1834).

The Lower Barracca ✣ ✣ (Valletta, map reference 47)

From Castile Square walk down St Paul's Street or St Ursula Street until you come to St Christopher Street; turn right towards the Harbour.

This garden at the lower end of Valletta is another favourite spot for relaxation. As in the case of the Upper Barracca it was a place of recreation for the Knights, and it was later used by the French as a market garden in order to feed their troops during the blockade of 1798-1800. Again we find several memorials, including one to Sir Alexander Ball, the first English Civil Commissioner in Malta (1798-1801). He played a leading part when combined Maltese and British forces defeated the French in Valletta.

Hastings Gardens

Enter Valletta through City Gate. Turn left at Ordinance Street and left again when you reach St John's Cavalier.

Another small but attractive garden forming part of St James's Bastion. The Gardens are named after the Marquess of Hastings who fought in the American War of Independence and was Governor of Malta during 1824-26. His monument is to be found in the centre of the garden. A fine panoramic view of Marsamxett Harbour can be had from here.

OUTSIDE VALLETTA

The Mall – Floriana

Not far from City Gate and the City Gate Bus Terminus, and a stone's throw from the Hotel Le Meridien Phoenicia, are the Maglio Gardens (The Mall). Converted into a public garden in 1805, it was previously an enclosure reserved for the Knights to play a ball-game called *pallamaglio*. The austere Grand Master who built the Maglio enjoined his Knights to play games in order to counteract the effects of wine, women and dice. Whether or not it served its purpose is a matter for conjecture. At the main entrance stands a statue commemorating Malta's Independence.

Argotti – Floriana ✣

Open daily from 8.30 a.m. to Sunset. Admission free.

At the back of the Mall is the entrance to another attractive garden known as the Argotti Botanic Gardens, which contains a large variety of rare plants, including a valuable collection of cacti.

A stone's throw from the main entrance to the Gardens stands Sarria Church built in 1585 and named after its founder, Martino de Sarria, a Knight of Navarre. It was enlarged in 1678 at the expense of Grand Master Rafael Cotoner and his knights in fulfilment of a vow following their deliverance from the plague of 1675-76.

Sa Maison – Floriana ✣

From City Gate bus terminus walk past the Hotel Le Meridien Phoenicia and Independence Arena; turn right at Britannia Street, left through St Calcedonius Square, and down Sa Maison Road. *Open 7 a.m. to 4.45 p.m. between October 1 and June 15. Admission free.*

Once a place of recreation for the Knights, the Sa Maison Nursery Gardens were skilfully re-planned by the British in the early 19th century. Look out for the tablets of carvings of British regiments associated with Malta which are to be found on the rock face. At the extreme end of the garden is an arch over nine metres wide joining two

MALTA and GOZO – Sun, Sea and History

Sarria Church, Floriana

bastions together. The curve is of a "tortuous and oblique form" much admired by connoisseurs. It was constructed by the Maltese engineer Vincenzo Barbara, who was also responsible for some of the fortifications which surround Floriana. The Gardens command an excellent view of Marsamxett Harbour.

Garden of Repose – Floriana ✥

Walk down Great Siege Road on the left of the Hotel Le Meridien Phoenicia and turn left heading towards the public lending library. (Open 9 a.m. to 5 p.m. Monday to Saturday; 1 p.m. in Summer)

This peaceful garden is to be found next to the Msida Bastion Cemetery which was the main Protestant cemetery for some fifty years from 1806. British servicemen, officials and businessmen are buried here, including John Hookham Frere and his wife the Dowager Countess of Erroll. Hookham Frere (1769-1846), a distinguished diplomat, classical scholar and prominent Freemason who came to Malta in 1821. Some Maltese, including Mikiel Anton Vassalli, known as the 'father of the Maltese language' who died in 1826, are also buried there. The bastions were built in the 17th century by the Italian engineer, Floriani, and were commissioned by Grand Master Antoine de Paule in 1635 as additional protection for the city of Valletta.

The cemetery was damaged during the Second World War but was restored and repaired by *Din L-Art Helwa* (see page 291). The visitor enters the Garden through a high gateway. A pair of George III cannon each weighing four tons have been mounted in embrasures to the right hand side.

President's Palace, San Anton, Attard

San Anton Palace and Gardens – Attard ✥✥

The Gardens are open daily from 7 a.m. to sunset. Admission free. City Gate Terminus, Lija Bus (No. 40). Ask the conductor to put you down near San Anton Palace.

The seventeenth century Palace[2] in Attard was originally the country seat of Grand Master Antoine de Paule, who despite his 72 years of age was determined to enjoy life to the full. He entertained 600 guests to a sumptuous dinner at San Anton on the day of his

---

[2] It is interesting to note that when Victor Emmanuel's troops were marching on Rome in 1862 the British Government offered to place San Anton Palace at the disposal of Pope Pius IX in case of need; an offer which did not please "The Times" of London.

WHAT TO SEE (6) – Gardens and Garden Centres

> Princess Victoria Melita, granddaughter of Queen Victoria was born at San Anton Palace, Malta, on November 25, 1875. Her parents were Prince Alfred, Duke of Edinburgh and the Grand Duchess Alexandrovna of Russia. The Princess married Ferdinand of Romania

installation and fell foul of the Inquisitor Fabio Ghigi (afterwards Pope Alexander VII) who complained to the Vatican of "his irreverence, sensuality and duplicity".

In 1810, Napoleon's brother, Lucien Bonaparte, was placed under "house arrest" here having been captured by the British while on his way to the United States from Rome. He was later taken to England aboard the frigate "President".

Today the Palace is the official residence of the President of the Republic.

The gardens, which are beautifully laid out, are open to the public, and contain a large quantity of trees, shrubs and plants. Well worth a visit.

Buskett – Outskirts of Rabat ✣✣

Open at all times and every day. Rabat bus (No. 80). Alight at Rabat Bus Terminus, then get a car or taxi, or walk via Nikol Saura Street and Buskett Road for a kilometre or so.

One of the beauty spots of the Island, "il-Buskett" ("Boschetto" – little wood), surrounds Verdala Castle. Here you will find gigantic ash trees, Aleppo pines and cypress tress, some evergreen oak and, of course, orange, lemon and olive trees. Originally planted by Grand Master Cardinal de Verdalle in the sixteenth century it is a little oasis.

Kennedy Memorial Grove – Salina ✣

The Kennedy Grove is best reached by car, although during the summer months a Sliema bus leaves the bus stop at Gżira, opposite

Manoel Island Bridge, every hour between 2 p.m. and 9 p.m. and goes to St Paul's Bay via Salina Bay.

Situated at Salina, the Kennedy Memorial Grove was opened on the 29th May, 1966 and is a memorial by the people of Malta to President John Fitzgerald Kennedy, who was assassinated in 1963. On the memorial are inscribed the words: "Ask not what your country can do for you; ask what you can do for your country".

Palazzo Parisio – Naxxar ✣✣

This is a stately 19th century Palazzo with a splendid garden in private family ownership, situated in Victory Square, Naxxar, opposite the Parish Church. Coffee and gift shops are included. Once the residence of Marquis Giuseppe Scicluna. *Opening hours Monday to Friday (except Public Holidays) 9 a.m. to 1 p.m. (last admission 1 p.m.). Guided tours on the hour. (Telephone 21412461) (Admission fee).*

The Chinese Garden of Serenity – Santa Lucia ✣

The Chinese Garden of Serenity in Santa Lucia was a gift of the Chinese Government to Malta made in 1997. A peaceful and well laid-out garden it is open from 8.15 a.m. to 4.30 in winter and 7.45 a.m. to 2 p.m. in summer. (Bus 1) (Santa Lucia Local Council, Telephone 21 666600).

Rundle Gardens – Victoria, Gozo ✣

The Villa Rundle Gardens at the start of the hill leading to the centre of Victoria (Rabat) are named after General Sir Leslie Rundle, British Governor of Malta between 1909 and 1915, and are the venue for the agricultural show held on the day of the feast of the Assumption (*Santa Marija*) in mid-August.

WHAT TO SEE (6) – Gardens and Garden Centres

Cemeteries

The Addolorata ✣

(Open Government hours, 8 a.m. to 4 p.m.)

The Santa Maria Addolorata Cemetery and Garden is situated at Tal Horr Hill, just past the town of Marsa. It is the main Catholic burial place and was designed by the Maltese architect Emanuele Galizia in 1863. The St Mary chapel built in the neo-Gothic style dominated the cemetery.

The Muslim cemetery nearby was also built to a design by Galizia in 1873.

Imtarfa Military Cemetery ✣

The Imtarfa Military Cemetery is looked after by the Commonwealth War Graves Commission. It is situated on the road leading to Rabat from Mosta and may be visited during weekends from 8.30 to dusk throughout the year. *Also Monday to Friday from 6.30 to 4.30 (April to June); 6.30 to 1 p.m. (July to September), and 6.30 to 4 p.m. (October to March). (Tel. 21580234)*

Other cemeteries which are looked after by the War Graves Commission are to be found at Kalkara, Pembroke and Pietà.

Ta' Braxia – Pietà ✣

The Ta' Braxia cemetery was opened in 1856 when the Msida Bastion was more or less full. The Ta' Braxia cemetery in Pietà, not far from Porte des Bombes, is also worth visiting and is undergoing restoration. It was designed by Maltese architect Emanuele Luigi Galizia who was responsible for the Catholic cemetery known as the *Addolorata Cemetery* which bears a close resemblance to the Nord Cemetery of Paris one of several cemeteries visited by Galizia before accepting the commission. Among those buried there is Andrew Moyinham who died in 1867 and who was awarded the Victoria Cross at the Siege of Sevastapole. (*Ta' Braxia is open daily from 8 a.m. to 4 p.m.*).

Jewish Cemeteries

A small Jewish cemetery in Rinella Street, Kalkara, first built in 1784, was being refurbished at the time of going to Press, and is being turned into a Museum. This will include the *tehira*, a room where the body of the deceased and the shroud were washed as part of the burial ritual. There are two other Jewish cemeteries, one at Marsa, which dates back to the mid-19th century, and one near Ta' Braxia cemetery, which is in a state of neglect.

Garden Centres

Interest in gardening has increased over the years and among leading garden centres are:

The Garden Shop Nursery (Peter Calamatta)

Triq San Ġwann tal-Għargħur, San Ġwann, (Tel. 21386830).

F. Zammit Nurseries

22 Valletta Road, Qormi, (Tel. 21487188) (Also the Kiosk in Republic Street, Valletta). (Interflora member)

WHAT TO SEE (6) – Gardens and Garden Centres

> **The Turkish Plot**
>
> In 1749 a conspiracy, known as the Turkish Plot, was hatched to get rid of Grand Master Manoel Pinto and take possession of the island. A certain Mustapha Pasha, a Muslim of some consequence, with the aid of slaves organised a plan which included the murder of the Grand Master and had every prospect of success. Following a quarrel in a coffee shop, the owner, Joseph Cohen, a Jew who had become a Christian, overheard the plotters and reported them to the Grand Master. Nearly 40 slaves were put to death. Cohen was awarded a house by the grateful Grand Master and an annuity of three hundred ducats. A tablet fixed to the wall of his house commemorated his action. This is now in the Museum of Archaeology in Valletta.

Flower Power

The Nursery, Ta' Qali, Mosta (Also open on Sunday) (Tel. 21436181).

Sherries Garden Centre

Burmarrad Road, Burmarrad (Tel. 21580021).

Jardinland Garden Centre

258 Triq il-Kbira, Mosta (Tel. 21414642).

Derek Garden Centre

11 Triq il-Kanun, Qormi (Tel. 21449754).

Pot and Plant

1 Triq San Pawl, San Ġwann (Tel. 21386481).

'Il-Qronfla', Lewis Micallef Co. Ltd.

'Il-Qronfla', 253, Main Street, Balzan (Tel. 21442193). (Interflora member)

What to See (7)

In the Footsteps of St Paul

> *Then cried the soul of the stout Apostle Paul to God:*
> *"Once we frapped a ship, and she laboured woundily.*
> *There were fourteen score of them,*
> *And they blessed Thee on their knees,*
> *When they learned Thy Grace and Glory*
> *under Malta by the sea!"*
>
> KIPLING

Paul of Tarsus, St Paul, Apostle of the Gentiles, was shipwrecked here in the year AD 60 while on his way to Rome to stand trial. Paul remained in Malta for three months, converted the island to Christianity, and cured the sick, among whom was the father of the Roman Governor, Publius. He left behind him a rich religious heritage, and the island, whose patron he is, is often referred to as the 'Island of St Paul'.

St Paul's Grotto

St Paul's Grotto, in Rabat, has long been a centre of worship, and tradition holds that it was here that the apostle was kept during his stay. The shrine has had several distinguished visitors including the Spanish nobleman and hermit, Juan Venegas de Cordoba. His dedication attracted the patronage of the Order of St John. Venegas acquired a unique collection of holy relics including a bone fragment of the arm of St Paul donated by Duke Ferdinand of Mantua in 1620. Works of art were commissioned, sacred vestments made, and indulgencies secured. In 1607 Venegas obtained the permission of Pope Pius V to look after the crypt and in 1167 the Grotto was handed over to Grand Master Alof de Wignacourt (1601-1622).

Within the Grotto is a marble statue of Paul donated by the Portuguese Grand Master, Manoel Pinto de Fonseca (1741-1773). Another artistic statue of the Apostle also in the Grotto is by the Maltese sculptor Melchiorre Gafà (1638-1667). Chippings from the rock were often taken away since it was claimed that these had supernatural qualities. But because of the description in the Acts of the Apostles (Chapter 28), which described how Paul remained unharmed when bitten by a viper, it was against snakebites and poison that the rock from the cavern achieved fame. Its properties were acclaimed in a book published in Venice in 1554.

The Sanctuary at Mellieħa

In the north-west of Malta lies the village of Mellieħa (*see map of Malta*). This is the most remote parish in the island and probably the first hamlet visited by Paul of Tarsus.

The village, which was subject to frequent raids by pirates, was all but abandoned in the fifteenth century. Mellieħa is also noted for the ancient sanctuary of the Blessed Virgin whose image to be found painted on the rock. This sanctuary is a semi-troglodyte church and is the oldest Marian sanctuary in the Maltese Islands. Among its distinguished visitors in days gone by were King Ferdinand and King Alfonso of Aragon. Any Maltese captured and sold into slavery, would vow to visit the sanctuary if and when winning his freedom. Pope John Paul II was a pilgrim in 1990.

WHAT TO SEE (7) – In the Footsteps of St Paul

St Paul's Island

St Paul's Island

St Paul was shipwrecked, together with 274 others in an area north-west of Malta where lies tiny St Paul's Island – 885 metres long and some 200 metres wide. The islet now uninhabited was once cultivated. In its centre stands a statue of the Apostle, the work of two Maltese sculptors in 1845 bearing an inscription in Latin which read: *'To the Apostle Paul, Master and Doctor and of all people, Father and Patron of the Maltese'*. 1960 being the 19th centenary of the famous shipwreck, a commemoration was held and attended by hundreds of the faithful while numerous traditional Maltese boats such as the *Dghajsa* and the *Luzzu*

The fishing 'luzzu'

surrounded the little island. In 1990, Pope John Paul II presided at a colourful ceremony when a large statue of Christ with outstretched arms was laid on the seabed in the island's vicinity. It will be familiar to divers.

See also:

The Cathedral in Mdina (page 94)

The Parish Church in Rabat (page 104)

The Anglican Cathedral in Valletta (page 62)

26. An effigy of St Paul at the entrance to Mdina

27. Maltese sunset – "Golden Glow"

28. The Temple of Mnajdra dating back to 2800BC and (*below*) The Hypogeum – one of the wonders of the world

29. Aerial view of the temple of Ħaġar Qim and (*below*) one of the statuettes found during excavations at the Brocktorff Circle in Xagħra, Gozo

30. The temple of Ġgantija in Gozo – older than Stonehenge and the Pyramids of Egypt and (*below*) the mysterious cart-ruts scattered all over the island

31. Striking aerial view of the Citadel in Gozo

32. Entrance to Fort Ricasoli at the mouth of Grand Harbour, built in 1694

33. Mosta church with its mighty dome claimed to be the third largest in the world

34. Portes des Bombes, Floriana (1721) and (*below*) the Courve Porte, Vittoriosa (1723)

35. Żabbar Gate, Cottonera

36. Courtyard, Inquisitor's Palace, Vittoriosa

37. The garden at San Anton and (*below*) one of several garden centres

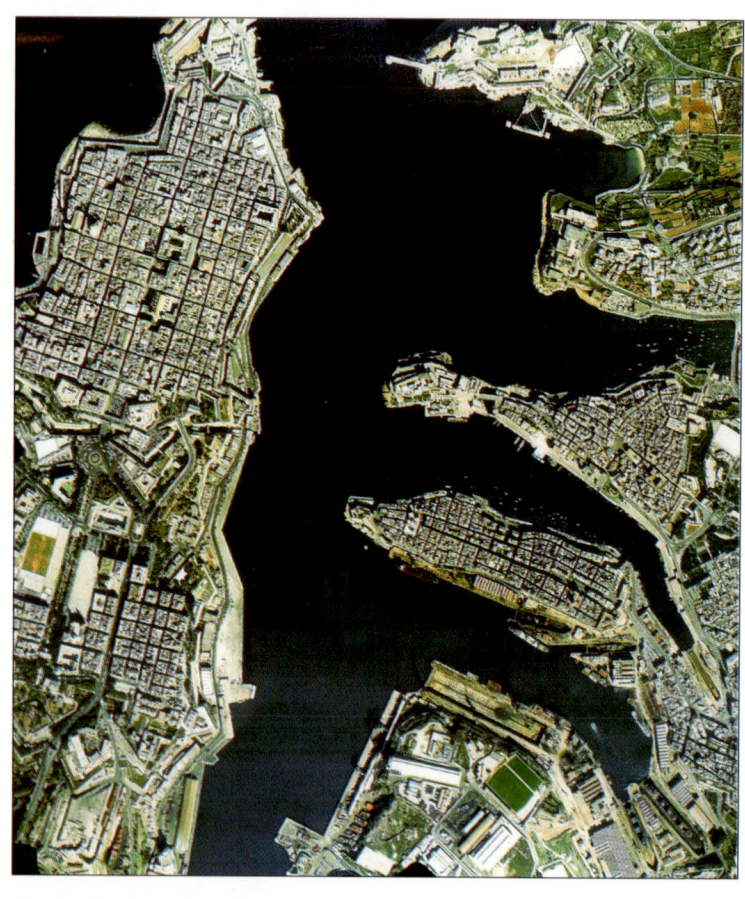

38. Aerial view of Valletta and Grand Harbour with Fort Ricasoli, Fort St Angelo, in Vittoriosa and Senglea

What to See (8)

Grand Harbour and Vittoriosa

The Grand Harbour is truly magnificent. Together with Marsamxett Harbour it affords deep and safe anchorage to the largest vessel. As far back as 325-260 B.C. the Roman, Diodorus Siculus, recorded that the Phoenicians found this 'a place of refuge, from the excellence of its harbours, and its situation in the middle of the sea'. It was its harbours which has made the island the object of fierce rival ambitions and has attracted the covetous eyes of maritime powers throughout the ages.

Napoleon was right when he said that a country's geography makes its history. Malta is what the sea and her harbours have made her.

Grand Harbour is surrounded by the bastions of Fort St Elmo, Ricasoli, and St Angelo and has four inner creeks – Rinella, Kalkara, Dockyard and French Creeks – all affording safe anchorage. Grand Harbour's shore line is 15.28 kilometres long and it encloses 540 acres of water, while Marsamxett Harbour claims 380 acres. Most of this area is more than four fathoms deep, and a substantial part of both harbours is over ten fathoms deep.

The harbours have seen much history and many fierce battles.

If you look across the Grand Harbour from the upper Barracca Gardens you will see the "Three Cities" of Vittoriosa ("Birgu"), Senglea ("L'Isla") and Cospicua

Vittoriosa

1. Oratory of St. Joseph
2. Auberge d'Alemagne
3. Auberge d'Angleterre
4. Auberge d'Auvergne et de Provence
5. Sacra Infermeria / Benedictine Nunnery
6. Auberge de France
7. 'Norman' House
8. Auberge de Castille et de Portugal
9. Armoury
10. St. James Cavalier
11. Bishop's Palace
12. Università Palace
13. Inquisitor's Palace
14. St. John Cavalier
15. Annunciation Church
16. Church of St. Lawrence
17. Freedom Monument
18. Maritime Museum
19. Treasury of the Order
20. Carmelite Church
21. Captain General's Palace
22. Auberge d'Italie
23. Fort St. Angelo
24. Site of Slave Prisons
25. Monserrat Church
26. Site of Auberge d'Aragon
27. St. Philip's Church

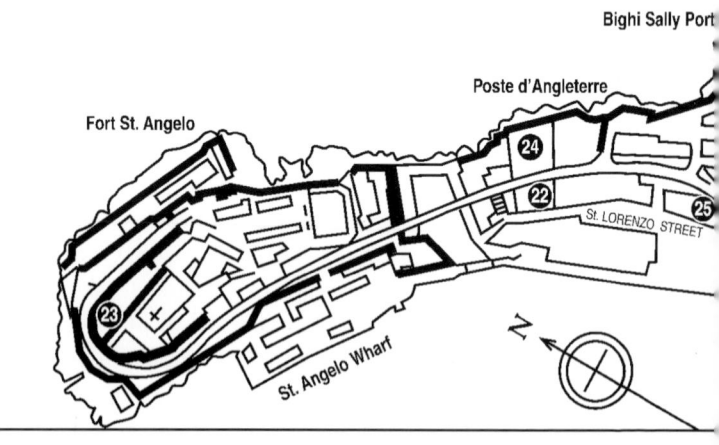

Plan of Vittoriosa (Birgu)

WHAT TO SEE (8) – Grand Harbour and Vittoriosa

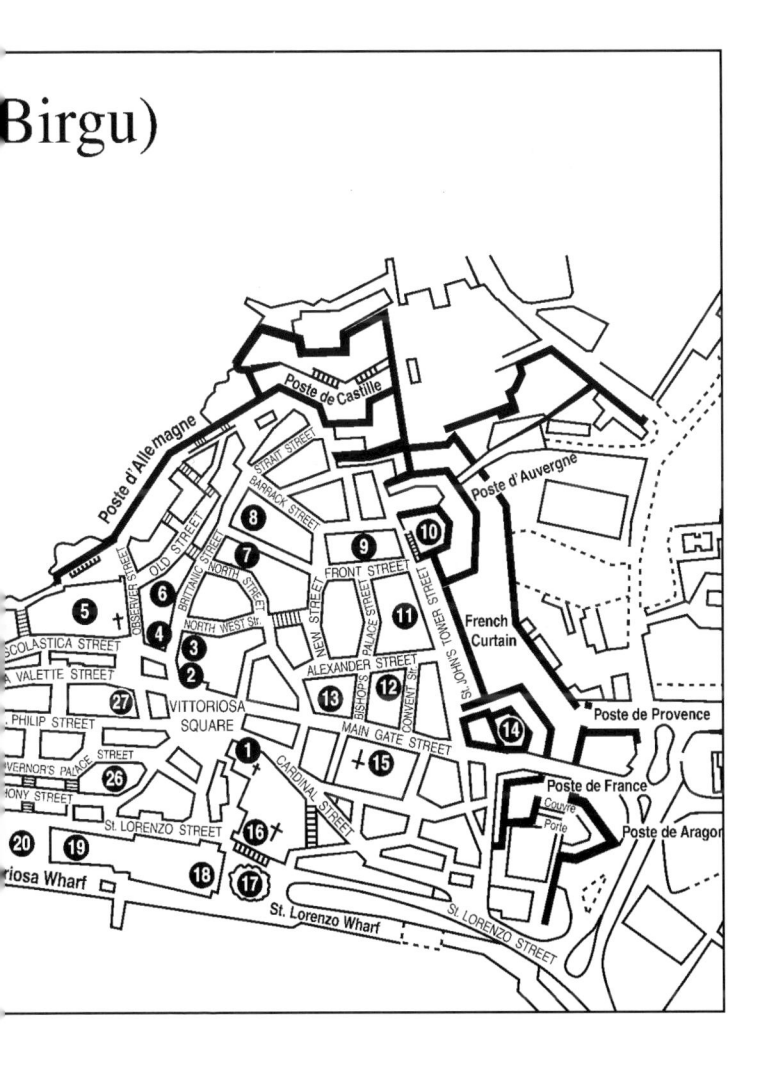

("Bormla") all of which are older than Valletta. Vittoriosa, the oldest of the three, was used by the Order of St John as their headquarters before Valletta was built, and received its name "The Victorious One" following the gallant part it played in the siege of 1565. It was again heavily damaged during the Second World War.

There are many places of historic interest here and these are often overlooked by the visitor. Here are some of the more prominent sites:

St Angelo ✥ (pages 168-169, Vittoriosa map, reference 23)

A part of Fort St Angelo is open to the public from June to September, Saturday 10 a.m. to 1 p.m.; October to May, Saturday 10 a.m. to 2 p.m.; (entrance fee also covers St Elmo. The best way to get to the Castle is by boat from Customs House Steps in Valletta; alternatively catch a bus to Vittoriosa.

Much of the Island's history has centred around Fort St Angelo – the "Castello a Mare". A temple to Astarte, the Phoenician Venus, and later a temple to the Roman Juno are believed to have stood on this site and it is also probable that a fort has existed here from very ancient times. A fort was certainly built by the Arabs in 828 and under Aragonese rule, St Angelo was the residence of the Nava family, Barons of Marsa. On the arrival of the Knights, Grand Master L'Isle Adam (1530-1534) strengthened the Fort and it soon became the centre of the Order's defensive system. The Fort was also used as a State prison of the Order. St Angelo was severely bombed during World War II, when it became HMS St Angelo, Headquarters of the Royal Navy and later of the Allied Forces, Mediterranean, with the flags of six of the NATO nations, Great Britain, France, Greece, Italy, Turkey and the U.S.A.

The upper part of St Angelo is leased to the Sovereign Military Order of St John and is normally closed to visitors.

WHAT TO SEE (8) – Grand Harbour and Vittoriosa

The Castle of St Angelo

There are two chapels in St Angelo, one dedicated to the Blessed Virgin dating back to 1090; the other dedicated to St Anne and rebuilt by L'Isle Adam in 1531. The Castle remained until 1979, H.M.S. St Angelo, Headquarters of the Commander British Forces, Malta.

Inquisitor's Palace ✥✥ (Vittoriosa map, reference 13)

City Gate Terminus. Cospicua Bus (No. 1). Alight at Bus Terminus and walk up the hill. Turn left into Main Gate Street, Vittoriosa, past the Dominican Church on your left. The Inquisitor's Palace is a few yards ahead on your right. 1st October to 15 June, Monday to Saturday 8.15 a.m. to 5 p.m.; Sunday 8.15 a.m. to 4.15 p.m.; 16 June to 30 September, daily 7.45 a.m. to 2 p.m. (Entrance fee). (Tel. 21663731)

This sixteenth century building, the *Palazzo del Santo Uffizio*, was used by the Inquisitors of the Holy Office as their residence, court and prison. It has a forbidding exterior but a lovely courtyard with pointed arches which is all that remains of an older building, the *Castellania*. The ceiling of the main hall is of carved wood with the coats of arms of the sixty-two Inquisitors who lived there. The post was an important one and of the sixty-two who held office in Malta, twenty-five were subsequently made Cardinals and two, Fabio Chigo and Antonio Pignatelli became Popes – Alexander VII (1655-67) and Innocent XII (1691-1700).

The Office of the Inquisitors, an Institution established by the Catholic Church to combat heresy, was set up in Malta following differences between Grand Master La Cassiere, a Frenchman, and the Spaniard Mgr. Martino Royas, Bishop of Malta. La Cassiere also wished to ensure that his Knights remained free from "the pestilential heresies" of the Reformation. But the arrival of the first Inquisitor, Mgr. Pietro Dusina in 1572, meant that the sovereign Grand Master had to face two separate and formidable rivals: the Bishop of Malta and the Grand Inquisitor. The followers of each – exempt from the jurisdiction of the other – were often at daggers drawn. This led to confusion, and many disputes had to be referred to the Pope for judgment. (*See page 110 for the Inquisitor's Summer Palace at Girgenti, not far from Verdala Castle near Buskett Gardens*).

Church of St Lawrence ✥✥ (Vittoriosa map, reference 16)

City Gate Terminus, Cospicua Bus (No. 1). Alight at bus terminus and enter Vittoriosa through St Lawrence Street.

The Parish Church of St Lawrence, the original Conventual Church of the Order of St John, dates back to Norman times but was rebuilt in 1691. Its treasury contains some interesting relics of the Order's days in Rhodes. In the nearby Oratory of St Joseph are the black silk hat and large sword used by Grand Master La Valette on the day of victory over the Turks. But the Jewelled sword given by

Philip II of Spain to the Grand Master is now in the Louvre, Paris, having been taken there by Napoleon. It was in this historic church that La Valette and his Knights prayed on the eve of the Great Siege in 1565, and here that they gave thanks and celebrated the lifting of the siege.

The first Auberges

When the Knights arrived in Malta from Rhodes the Order consisted of nine Langues all with their own modest auberges some of which are now private residences. The Auberge of England (*Vittoriosa map, reference 3*) was acquired by Sir Clement West and it now houses a public library. It is in Mistral Street.

The French Knights had an Auberge (*Vittoriosa map, reference 6*) in Hilda Tabone Street which was used as a Primary School and then as a carpenter's shop. Later still it was turned into a Museum of Political History which has since closed.

What remains of the Auberge of Germany (*Vittoriosa map, reference 2*) is to be found in Victory Square.

The Maritime Museum ✥✥

Not yet a centre of tourism, Vittoriosa is replete with history and will give enjoyment to those who are interested in the past. Vittoriosa Wharf is of special interest. Here is the Maritime Museum which features a good collection of model ships and many other exhibits dealing with the long maritime history of the island from the Phoenicians to the British period and the Royal Navy.

William Scamp, the British architect designed the Royal Navy's bakery on the site of the arsenal (*Vittoriosa map, reference 18*) of the Knights (1557). It became a Maritime Museum in 1992.

Maritime Museum, Vittoriosa

Opening hours: 1st October to 15 June, Monday to Saturday 8.15 a.m. to 5 p.m.; Sunday 8.15 a.m. to 4.15 p.m.; and June 16 to 30 September daily 7.45 a.m. to 2 p.m. (Entrance fee).

Also along the waterfront is the Scamp Palace once used by the Captain General of the Order. Severely damaged during the Second World War it has now been repaired and is used as a gaming Casino.

Villa Bighi in Kalkara

Across Rinella Bay from Fort Ricasoli stands a villa built by a knight of Malta, Fra Mario Bighi in 1675. During the British period several additions were made and the building used as a naval hospital. It is now utilised as a Discovery and Archaeology Resources Centre, partly, as a seat for the Council for Science and Technology and partly as a Centre for Restoration, an agency entrusted with the conservation and restoration of the islands' cultural heritage. (*Telephone 21823290*)

Exhibition Hall

An Exhibition Hall and Art Gallery, the *Gallerija Courve Port* is to be found on the ground floor of the building housing the Vittoriosa local Council, Courve Porte (Telephone 21662166).

(*For a tour of the Harbour see page 253*)

The Maid of Mosta

One of the island's many traditions and legends relates how in 1526 a party of marauders from the North African coast landed at Salina and sleathily made their way to the village of Mosta, guided by a renegade servant. They arrived at a house where a wedding was to take place of a beautiful maiden, Marianna Cumbo by name, who was betrothed to Antonio Manduca from Notabile (Mdina). After a brief sortie with loyal servants, Marianna was kidnapped and taken aboard ship to Tripoli where she was presented to the Pasha who added her to his harem. Marianna refused his advances and legend has it that her fiancée arrived in Tripoli and with the help of the Pasha's daughter, rescued his beloved and took her back to Malta where there was much rejoicing. Alas, legend has it that Marianna died before the wedding could take place.

Other Places of Interest

Buġibba and Qawra

Both Buġibba and Qawra have become popular holiday resorts.

At Buġibba the promenade along the waterfront offers watersports, cafes, restaurants, a cinema and lively nightlife. Qawra is quieter. The Qawra Tower at the tip of the peninsular was built in the 17th century by Grand Master de Redin. Those interested in archaeology will want to view the ancient megalith which stands in the garden of the New Dolmen Hotel. The Suncrest Hotel faces Salina Bay with its ancient salt pans, and another large hotel the Grand Hotel Mercure Coralies San Antonio in Triq it-Turisti, Qawra, has recently opened its doors (Telephone 21583434).

Mosta Church ✜✜✜

Open daily from 6 to 10.30 a.m. and from 3 to 7 p.m. City Gate Terminus. Mosta Bus (No. 53) alight at Mosta Terminus.

This large and imposing Church in Mosta, was built by voluntary labour and contributions between 1883 and 1863. Its dome is said to be the third largest in the world. Higher internally than the Pantheon in Rome and larger in diameter than the dome of St Paul's in London, it is surpassed only by St Peter's in Rome and St Sophia in Constantinople. It is estimated that Mosta Church can hold a standing congregation of 10,000. The Church was

The 'Rotunda' Church at Mosta

designed by the Maltese architect, Giorgio Grognet de Vasse. During the Second World War a large bomb came through the great dome as the congregation prepared for Mass. Fortunately it failed to explode and can now be seen in the sacristy.

Wied Iż-Żurrieq – The Blue Grotto ✥✥

Take a car to Wied Iż-Żurrieq, or a No. 32 bus from Valletta, then hire a boat to the Blue Grotto. The best time for a visit is the morning, but first check weather conditions (Police Station: 21826947).

Wied Iż-Żurrieq is a picturesque spot and the nearby

Blue Grotto which rivals the famous Blue Grotto in Capri, Italy, is an added attraction. Legend has it that the Grotto was a favourite meeting place for sirens who held seafarers spell-bound with their midnight songs. If you look down into the water you will see a brilliant blue phosphorescent light. There are several smaller caves (including *Għar Qattus*, "Cat's Cave") also worth a visit. You can only reach the Blue Grotto by boat. Not far from Blue Grotto is Babu Valley (*Wied Babu*) another beauty spot for lovers of nature.

The Blue Grotto, Zurrieq

Siġġiewi – 'Heritage in Stone' ✣✣

A new and unusual attraction has come into being lately: It is the 'Limestone Heritage' which offers an insight into the ancient craft of quarrying and masonry. A multi-lingual video production gives an introduction to the subject; there is also an interesting collection of artifacts and machinery.

Situated at Mikiel Azzopardi Street Siġġiewi. Open from 9 a.m. to 3 p.m. Monday to Friday, and between 9 a.m. and Noon on Saturday and Sunday. (Tel. 21464931). No 89 bus from Valletta.

Malta Aviation Museum, Ta' Qali ✣

The Aviation Museum is situated near the Crafts Village at Ta' Qali. *Opening Hours 9 a.m. to 5 p.m. except on Good Friday, Easter Sunday, Christmas Eve and Christmas Day and New Year's Day (Tel. 21416095).* The first flight recorded at Malta took place on February 13, 1915 when a biplane from HMS Ark Royal, berthed in Grand Harbour, and flew over the island for a few minutes. During the 1920's and 1930's Malta was a staging post for many aviation pioneers. The Air Battles of Malta during World War II was another milestone in Malta's aviation history. The Museum has reached the first phase of this ambitious project, run by volunteers. (Entrance fee).

Ħal Millieri Medieval Chapel ✣✣

Follow the main road from the Malta International Airport, Gudja, to Żurrieq, turn right at signpost to Ħal Millieri. *Open every Sunday between 10 a.m. and Noon.*

This siculo-normal Chapel of the Annunciation was built late in the 14th or early in the 15th century and is one of the few remaining relics of Medieval Malta. Surrounded

Medieval Chapel of Ħal Millieri

by its own churchyard, in unspoilt countryside between Żurrieq and Mqabba, the Chapel marks the site of the old deserted village of Ħal Millieri. Its twelve frescoes[1] are of special historic and artistic interest, and they still show signs of high craftsmanship. Stylistically primitive, the Chapel consists of a low rectangular nave bridged by four pointed arches dividing it into five bays. The upkeep of Ħal Millieri Chapel is the responsibility of *Din l-Art Ħelwa* (see page 291) whose members spent a great deal of time cleaning the Chapel, long disused, and restoring some of its pristine beauty.

---

[1] Other medieval frescoes are to be found in the Chapel of St Mary (page 187) and in the troglodyte Chapel of St Agatha (page 108).

Għadira Nature Reserve ✢✢

The Għadira Nature Reserve (next to Mellieħa Bay, *see Map of Malta*) is a haven for migrating birds and a refuge for all those seeking peace and quiet. BirdLife Malta is responsible for the Reserve which is open to the public between mid-October and the end of May. Opeb on Saturdays and Sundays from 9.30 am to 3.30 pm, in December and January, and from 10.30 am to 4.30 pm between February and May. Besides birds there are rabbits, weasels, hedgehogs, the westen whip snake and the chameleon. One tree planted in the area is the Sandarac Gum Tree which has been chosen as the island's national tree. (BirdLife Tel. 21347646)

Ħal Far – Ħasan's Cave

City Gate Terminus. Kalafrana (bus no. 12). Alight at Kalafrana and then follow the sign posts. Entrance free. (Take a torch with you).

This large cave on the south-eastern cliffs of the Island is said to have been used as a hiding place by a Saracen named Ħasan, who hid there with his girlfriend to evade expulsion in 1120. It is 200 feet above sea level and has three interior passages leading from its entrance.

Off the Beaten Track

Cliffs and Countryside

Most visitors tend to concentrate on the towns. Because of lack of time or because they feel there is nothing worth seeing they often ignore the countryside. True, the first impression especially in summer is one of barrenness and of innumerable rubble walls. But at the right time of the year there is much which is beautiful off the beaten track.

The best time for country excursions is from late October, after the first rainfall, until April when the orange blossom is in bloom, and the best way to see the countryside is on foot. It is more rewarding to discover these places for yourself; I will merely give an indication of the areas where you can find the most striking of the rugged cliff scenery and of the countryside with its fertile valleys (*widien*).

During your walks you will come across the hardy and indigenous carob and fig trees, the ubiquitous prickly pear, the ancient vine and olive tree and even, if you go to Wardija or Buskett, the large evergreen oak (*ballut*). In March and April you will see fields crimson with clover (*silla*) with which many acres are sown for fodder.

You will come across little farmhouses; picturesque rural Chapels, busy windmills and isolated gateways many of them with armorial emblems; archaeological remains: countless niches, for the Maltese are a religious people; towers and forts, reminders of pirates and corsairs who came to plunder; and finally sweet smelling narcissi, poppies, and the wild caper. All these you will see if you seek them out.

A wayside Chapel

No Sanctuary

When strolling in the country the visitor may come across a small marble slab on the external wall of chapels bearing this inscription:

NON GODE
IMMUNITA'
ECCLESIASTICA

The inscription means that the church in question does not enjoy the right of ecclesiastical sanctuary. Up to the beginning of the 19th century Ecclesiastical Courts in Malta exercised temporal jurisdiction over the clergy. This jurisdiction extended over all consecrated buildings; and sometimes criminals, and others, sought refuge, and the civil authorities could do nothing about it. The right to sanctuary was abused and the Church tried to control it by fixing the above notice on various rural churches. Ponsonby, a British Governor, abolished the right in 1818.

Cottonera & Margherita Lines

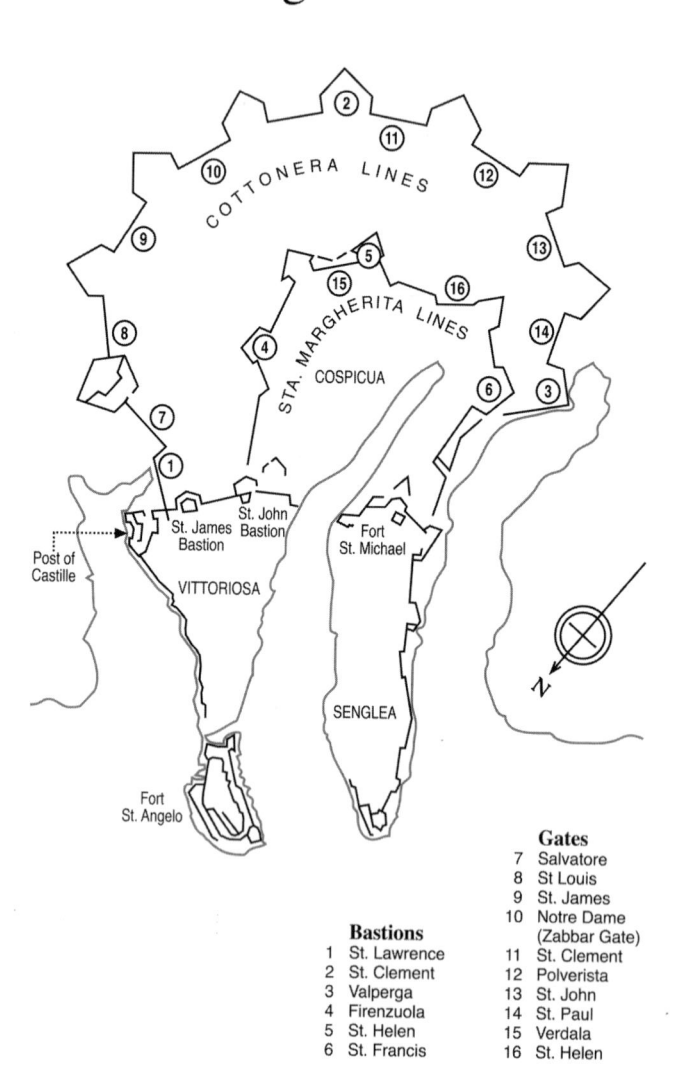

Bastions
1. St. Lawrence
2. St. Clement
3. Valperga
4. Firenzuola
5. St. Helen
6. St. Francis

Gates
7. Salvatore
8. St Louis
9. St. James
10. Notre Dame (Zabbar Gate)
11. St. Clement
12. Polverista
13. St. John
14. St. Paul
15. Verdala
16. St. Helen

OFF THE BEATEN TRACK

Walks and Excursions

Here are some suggested areas for walks and excursions together with a few notes on places of special interest.

(1) *To Mtaħleb – Baħrija – Kunċizzjoni – Binġemma*

The Roman Museum in Rabat is a good starting point for walks into the country. If you take the road to the left of the Museum, and make your way to the small pumping station at Għajn Qajjied, you will be able to follow the sign posts to any one of five rural villages: Mtaħleb (and the valley of Miġra Ferħa); Baħrija (and Baħrija Valley); Kunċizzjoni; Binġemma and Dwejra (follow the road sign to Tas-Salib for these last two).

NOTE: Wied Miġra Ferħa is where Roger the Norman is said to have landed in 1090 *(See "History in Brief")*.

(2) *To The Victoria Lines*

Both Binġemma and Dwejra are good starting points to explore the Dwejra and Victoria Lines. These lines of defences were built by the British between 1870 and 1899 (see pages 38-42 and Map of Malta on inside front cover) and cut across the Island from Fomm ir-Riħ Bay in the West. They are 12 kilometres in length.

(3) *To Fomm ir-Riħ Bay*

From Mtaħleb walk across to Wied Markozz; follow coast line towards Rdum tal-Vigarju; Wied tal-Baħrija and Fomm ir-Riħ Bay.

(4) *To Chadwick "Lakes"*

Mosta Church; walk through Main Street to Hope Street; Ta' l-Isperanza Bridge; Ta' l-Isperanza Valley; through Qlejgħa Valley to Chadwick "Lakes".

NOTE: Look out for the Chapel of Good Hope (*ta' l-Isperanza*) when you pass under the bridge to get into the valley. Beneath this Chapel is a Grotto, where according to tradition a young girl was miraculously sheltered from Turkish Corsairs who had landed at Salina Bay. A thick curtain of cobwebs, quickly formed across the mouth of the cave, thus deceiving her pursuers.

(5) *Ta' San Martin*

Wardija; Wied Qannotta; San Martin.

NOTE: At Wardija where Publius is reputed to have had a Villa in Roman times, look out for the seventeenth century Chapel of the Forsaken ("Madonna tal-Abbandunati"), built in 1690 by Ramon Perellos y Roccaful who later became Grand Master. The Chapel is attached to the "Castello tas-Sultan", which is of much older vintage and which was used by the Grand Master as his hunting lodge.

    The Chapel of St Martin, at nearby San Martin, overlooking the fertile Pwales Valley is also of ancient foundation and the present structure dates back to around 1600.

(6) *To Girgenti (Inquisitor's Summer Place)*

Dingli; Buskett: Dingli Cliffs; Girgenti.

NOTE: In a little valley near Dingli is the charming estate of *Djar il Bniet*, (literally, "The House of the Girls"), the oldest territorial fief in Malta. It belongs to the Inguanez family having been given to one of them by King Louis of the House of Aragon in 1350. According to a legend, there was once a cave here with cool running water and some young girls who went inside were never seen again.

The Inquisitor's attractive summer Palace at the head of a fertile valley at Girgenti was built in 1625 by Mgr. Honoratus Visconti. Attached to it is a little Chapel dedicated to St Charles Borromeo. (Not normally open to the public.)

(7) *To Għar Dalam*

Start at Gudja; Wied Ħas-Saptan; Wied Dalam; Għar Dalam. (Cave and Museum)

NOTE: Near Gudja, just off the road leading to Luqa, is the ancient Church of St Mary ("Ta' Bir Miftuħ") founded in 1436 and one of the Island's first Parish churches.

"Villa Bettina"

Also on the outskirts of Gudja, at Ix-Xlejli, is the early eighteenth century Dorell Palace, more commonly known as "Villa Bettina", now a private residence.

The Villa was built in 1770 by Bettina Muscati, Maltese aristocrat, who married the Marchese Dorell, a Frenchman of the *ancient regime*. Madame Bettina, who moved freely in international circles of elegance and intrigue, was Lady-in-Waiting to Caroline, wife of King Ferdinand of Naples. But the Queen became jealous of her and Marchesa Dorell was forced to return to Malta. "Bettina" is said to have welcomed Napoleon's invasion of Malta and to have entertained him at Gudja. She later became disillusioned with the French and placed her Palace at Gudja at the disposal of Colonel Thomas Graham, (later General Lord

Medieval Chapel of Bir Miftuh

Lynedoch) who was in command of the Anglo-Maltese forces opposing the French, and who set up his military headquarters there.

On the 4th May, 1800, Nelson's flagship the *Foudroyant* anchored off Malta with Sir William and Lady Hamilton as passengers. Nelson and his party were entertained at San Anton Palace by Captain (later Sir Alexander) Ball and at Villa Bettina by Colonel Graham. The *Foudroyant* left Malta with the same passengers aboard on May 20th.

A number of *Countryside Walks* published by the Tourism Authority are on sale from Booksellers. At the time of going to Press five had been published. *The Dwejra Lines Walk; The Girgenti Walk; The Bahrija Walk; The Marfa Ridge Walk; and Tas-Silg Walk*. (*See pages 203-204 for walks in Gozo*).

Island of Gozo

Three to four miles to the north-west of Malta is the smaller sister Island of Gozo. (Għawdex – pronounced *"Awdesh"* – to the Gozitans and the Maltese). Peaceful, less sophisticated and more fertile than Malta, Gozo is 14.50 kilometres long and eight kilometres wide, with a population of some 27,000 occupied mainly in farming, fishing and lace-making.

By and large, the history of Gozo is similar to that of Malta and much that is written in this guide book applies to Gozo. But its isolation – Gozitans complain it is the Cinderella of the Maltese Islands – has bred a certain charm and a resilience in its people which give it a character and a flavour all of its own.

Gozo is very much an Island of legend and myth, and it is here that the nymph Calypso is said to have lived, and here that she offered Ulysses immortality if he would stay with her forever. As it was, he is said to have been detained by Calypso for seven years before being released by command of Jupiter and returning to his faithful wife, Penelope

From early morning until late at night car ferries make regular 30-minute crossings between Ċirkewwa in Malta and Mġarr in Gozo. There is no ticket office in Malta: you pay at Mġarr before making your return journey. Buses from the City Gate terminus in Valletta connect with the ferries. (Telephone 21556114 for time-table). There is also a helicopter service between Malta's International Airport and Gozo's Heliport (Telephone 21557905). There are buses at Mġarr to coincide with the arrival of the ferry.

MALTA and GOZO – Sun, Sea and History

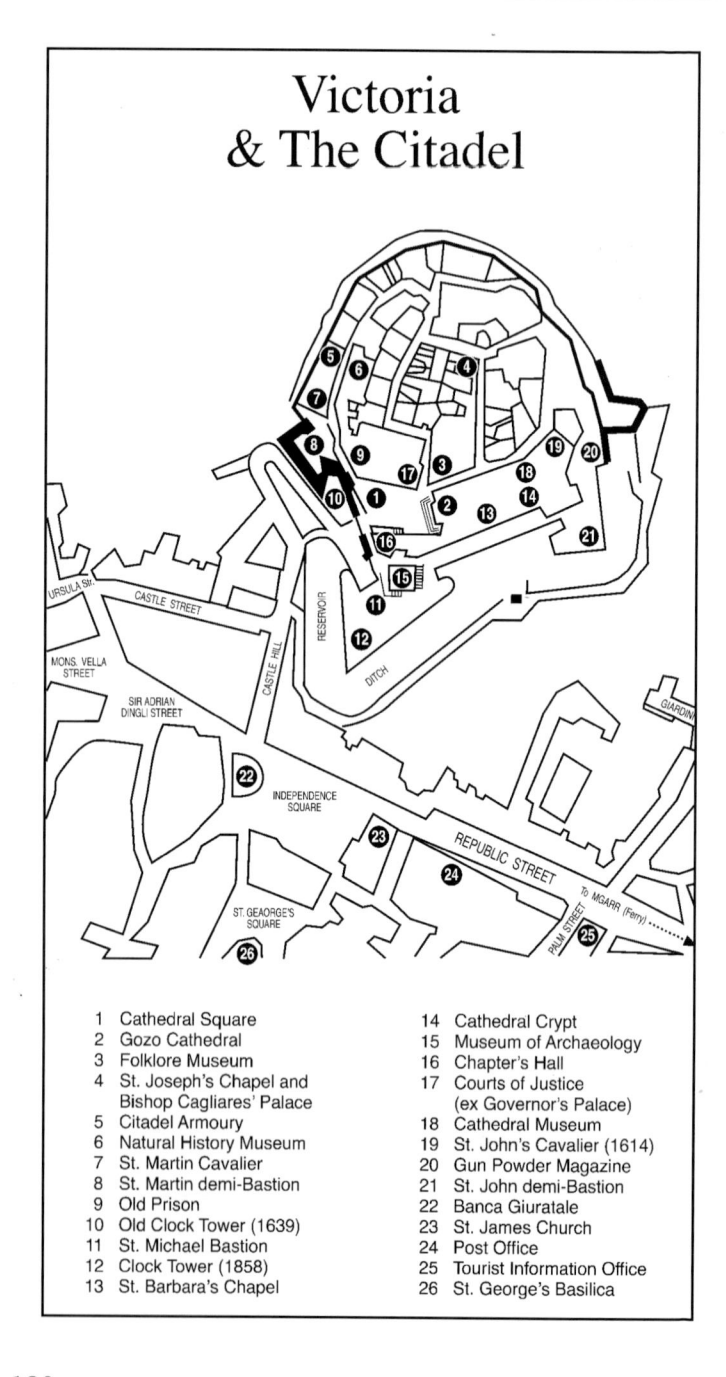

Victoria & The Citadel

1. Cathedral Square
2. Gozo Cathedral
3. Folklore Museum
4. St. Joseph's Chapel and Bishop Cagliares' Palace
5. Citadel Armoury
6. Natural History Museum
7. St. Martin Cavalier
8. St. Martin demi-Bastion
9. Old Prison
10. Old Clock Tower (1639)
11. St. Michael Bastion
12. Clock Tower (1858)
13. St. Barbara's Chapel
14. Cathedral Crypt
15. Museum of Archaeology
16. Chapter's Hall
17. Courts of Justice (ex Governor's Palace)
18. Cathedral Museum
19. St. John's Cavalier (1614)
20. Gun Powder Magazine
21. St. John demi-Bastion
22. Banca Giuratale
23. St. James Church
24. Post Office
25. Tourist Information Office
26. St. George's Basilica

The Legend of San Dimitri

Among the Legends of Gozo is that of San Dimitri. An old woman deeply grieved the loss of her only son – carried into captivity by the Turks – prayed at the little chapel of St Dimitrius for his return and promised she would keep an oil lamp burning in his Chapel from morning till night. Her prayer was answered and the Saint appeared on his charger with her son – the horse leaving hoofmarks on the edge of the cliff where the Chapel stood. The fifteenth century Chapel fell into the sea when Gozo was shaken by an earthquake, but on clear nights fishermen say they can still see the light burning in the Chapel on the sea bed.

(The present Chapel of San Dimitri was built in 1800 and is to be found at Birbuba, limits of Għarb)

From the bus terminus in Victoria (at Triq Putirjal); buses leave half an hour before all ferry departures between 6 a.m. to 7 p.m. – and later during the Summer months. There are taxi ranks at Mġarr, next to the Victoria bus terminus. (It is best to negotiate the fare in advance of your journey.)

There are tourist Information Offices at Mġarr Harbour (Telephone 21553343) and in Piazza Indipendenza in Victoria (Telephone 21558106).

You cross over to Gozo from Ċirkewwa (near Marfa, see page 204) and land at the picturesque harbour of Mġarr. Overlooking Mġarr is Fort Chambray, built to defend Gozo in 1749, and the Lourdes Sanctuary built in 1888.

You get to Rabat, the capital, some three miles inland, by bus or taxi.

Rabat – renamed Victoria on the occasion of Queen Victoria's Jubilee in 1887 – lies in the centre of the Island and is a good base for exploring the Island.

MALTA and GOZO – Sun, Sea and History

The Citadel, Gozo

WHAT TO SEE

The Castello (The Citadel) ✢✢

To get to the Citadel (street map of Victoria and The Citadel, page 190), turn right at the Main Square, Pjazza Indipendenza, in Rabat ("It-Tokk") and walk up Castle Hill.

Victoria is in fact a suburb of the *Castello* where all Gozitans sought refuge during the frequent attacks by the Turks and Corsairs who devastated and plundered the Island. In 1551, for example, Gozo was attacked by a combined force under Turkish General Sinan Pasha and the notorious Corsair, Dragut. The Citadel was sacked. Dragut's brother had been killed in a previous attack on Gozo in 1544 and his corpse burnt by the exasperated Gozitans. Dragut[1] swore to destroy the Island and in the attack of 1551 nearly six thousand men, women and children were taken into captivity. Many were eventually ransomed, but despite efforts to strengthen its defences Gozo remained vulnerable, and up to the beginning of the seventeenth century, it was the custom for all the inhabitants to seek refuge in the Citadel after dusk.

The Cathedral ✢✢

Many of the buildings in the Castello are in ruins, but some remain, and among these is the Cathedral (*Victoria & The Citadel map, reference 2*). Like Mdina in Malta, the Castello was inhabited from the earliest times and the Cathedral is said to have been built on a site once used as a temple to the Phoenician goddess, Astarte. The present Cathedral

---

[1] Dragut (known to the Turks as Turgut Reis) was himself killed in Malta during the Great Siege of 1565.

The Cathedral, Gozo

was designed by Lorenzo Gafà and was built between 1697 and 1711. The Cathedral has no dome; instead it has a striking painting by Antonio Manuele which gives the impression that a dome does in fact exist. The baptisimal font near the main entrance is of marble (alabaster) quarried from the village of Żebbuġ in Gozo. The quarry was discovered in 1738 but is now no longer in use.

Also in the Citadel are the Law Courts, built by Grand Master Wignacourt at the start of the seventeenth century; the Public Registry which up to 1551 was used as the residence of the Governor ("Ħakem") of Gozo, some medieval houses and the Museums.

ISLAND OF GOZO

> **Bernard the Brave**
>
> In one of the narrow lanes in the Citadel, stood the house of Bernard, who put up a fierce resistance to the Turkish attack in 1551. When he saw that the fortress could hold out no longer against overwhelming odds, Bernard took the life of his wife and two daughters rather than allow them to fall into the hands of the enemy. He himself fell, fighting to the end. A marble plaque commemorates the event.

St George's Basilica ✤✤

St George's Basilica (*Victoria map, reference 26*) in Victoria (Rabat) was built between 1672 and 1678 and stands at the centre of a patchwork of narrow streets in St George's Square. It has many works of art. The dome and the ceilings are by the Roman artist Giovanni Conti. Paintings by Mattia Preti and Stefano Erardi are also to be found here. Take note of the wooden statue of St George carved in 1841 by Paolo Azzopardi.

The Museums

The Museum of Archaeology, the Folklore Museum and the National History Museum (*Victoria & The Citadel map, references 15, 3 and 6 respectively*) are all in the Citadel.

Opening hours: Monday to Saturday, 8.30 a.m. to 4.30 p.m.; Sunday 8.30 to 3 p.m.

The Museum was formerly known as Palazzo Bondi and now contains some interesting archaeological finds which include Roman remains.

After visiting the Museum, walk round the ramparts which afford a marvelous panorama of the island.

Victoria (Rabat)

In Victoria's Main Square is the *Banca Giuratale* (Town Hall) (*Victoria & The Citadel map, reference 22*) built in 1773 and now used by Government Departments.

Also in the Main Square is the Church of St James. The original church was completely destroyed by the Turks in 1551 and the present building dates back to 1740. It is from this Church that the Island's crops are blessed each year on the 24th April, the feast of St Mark.

The bronze statue of Christ, also in the Square, is a Memorial to those who fell during the Second World War. It was unveiled by Queen Elizabeth in May 1954. An open air market adds colour to the scene in this Square.

In Republic Street leading to the Main Square is the Bishop's Palace (1880), the duke of Edinburgh Hotel, and next to the Hotel, the Rundle Gardens opened in 1914 by the British Governor Sir Leslie Rundle. The Gardens are open to the public, and an Agricultural Show is held there on the 14th and 15th August.

Ġgantija Temples ✥✥✥

The Ġgantija Temples are open at the same time as the Gozo Museum. *Open Monday to Saturday 8.30 a.m. to 4.30 p.m. Sunday 8.30 a.m. to 3 p.m. (Buses 64 or 65).*

Near the village of Xagħra are to be found the remains of the massive prehistoric temples of Ġgantija. These are somewhat similar to those at Mnajdra in Malta but both the areas enclosed, and the stone walls, are larger in the Gozo temple. This Neolithic temple which dates back to 3,600 B.C. is probably the finest and oldest in the Maltese Islands.

The admission ticket to the ancient temple also gives entry to the nearby windmill *il-Mitħna ta' Kola*, built in 1725 and recently restored. Its original wooden machinery is still there, as are tools of many trades and a forge.

Ġgantija Temple

Ta' Pinu Basilica ✢✢

Close to the village of Għarb is the famous and lovely Church of Ta' Pinu, dedicated to the Blessed Virgin. Long a place of devotion and piety the original chapel (now incorporated in the Basilica) dates back to the early fifteenth century. In 1883 a peasant woman, Carmela Grima (whose house can still be seen in Għarb) reported having heard the Blessed Virgin while praying in the old Chapel of Ta' Pinu. There followed reports of numerous cures and to mark these events the foundation stone of the present Church was laid on the 30th May, 1920.

Marble, life-size representations of the 'Way of the Cross' are positioned outside the church.

The Xewkija Rotunda ✣✣

Xewkija is one of the oldest villages in Gozo. After the war it was decided that the church of St John was not large

Dwejra, Gozo

enough and that a new one dedicated to St John the Baptist should be built. The first stone was laid down in 1951 and the new edifice was inspired by the design of the church of *Santa Maria della Salute* in Venice. It was built by voluntary labour and funded by weekly contributions from the village's 300 or so families. Donations also came from men and women who had emigrated to Australia and elsewhere. It was completed in 1978, and its impressive dome is one of the largest in the world.

For 50 cents a hydraulic lift takes visitors up on the roof for a panoramic view of the island.

Stalactite Caves

Not far from Xagħra and commanding a magnificent view of Ramla Bay are the so called caves of Calypso. Gozo is held by some to be the island of Ogygia described in Homer's Odyssey.

Qawra and Dwejra ✣✣

Some of the finest coastal scenery with complex geological faults is to be found in the north-western part of Gozo, and in particular around Qawra and Dwejra. Qawra is a small inland sea the origin of which is due to a peculiar pattern of faulting. Water and fishing boats enter by a 61 metre long fissure in the rock and the crystal-clear water makes Qawra Bay attractive to swimmers.

Beyond the little chapel of St Anne above the inland sea is the "Azure window" (*Tieqa Żerqa*) a massive sea-formed archway jutting out from the cliff. Nearby is the almost circular lagoon of Dwejra.

Both bays are guarded by Qawra Tower built in 1651.

MALTA and GOZO – Sun, Sea and History

Ta' Pinu Church

Fungus Rock ✢

The entrance to Dwejra Bay is almost blocked by a precipitous islet known as Fungus Rock, which gets its name from a scaly plant some 16cm in height which grows on its summit. Its astringent properties were in great demand during the days of the Order. Dried, powdered and mixed with wine or honey the plant was regarded as a quick acting remedy against dysentery, haemorrhage and ulcers. According to one historian it was also used for "superstitious and immoral" purposes.

The Grand Masters reserved to themselves the sole right to gather it and the punishment for transgressors was a spell in the galleys. Apparently this was an insufficient deterrent and in 1744 Grand Master Pinto instructed his engineers to make the rock as inaccessible as possible.

As late as 1824 the islet was still being visited for the plant and access to Fungus Rock was by means of a box suspended on pulleys and ropes stretched between the Rock and the mainland. Nowadays if you want to have a look at the plant (between January and May) and the lizards with green and yellow spots which allegedly live there, you will have to climb thirty metres of rock.

18th Century Windmills ✢

In the days of the Order of St John, windmills played an important part in the life of the community. Bread was a vital necessity and imported grain had to be milled into flour for the daily needs of the people and stored for times of siege.

Practically every town and village had its windmill: a quadrangular building erected round and incorporating a circular stone tower about fifteen metres high and three metres in diameter. On top of the tower – which also served as a look-out – were fixed six sails made of locally spun cotton. These turned the massive grindstones.

When the Knights left in 1798 there were twenty-six windmills in the Maltese Islands. Today only two remain in working order and both of these are to be found in Gozo. The one in operation, complete with sails and rigging, and still used for its original purpose is in an alley off Dalelands Street, in Qala; the other, built in 1725, is to be found near the Parish Church in Xagħra.

Museums

The Kelinu Grima Maritime Museum in Nadur. *Opening hours Monday to Saturday 9 a.m. to 4.45 p.m. Closed on Sunday and Public Holidays. (Entrance fee).*

The Pomskizillious Museum of Toys in Xagħra, *Opening hours Monday to Saturday 10 a.m. to Noon and 3 p.m. to 6 p.m. Mid October to April Saturday only 10 a.m. to 1 p.m.*

The Għarb Folklore Museum in the village of Għarb *Opening hours Monday to Saturday 9 a.m. to 4 p.m. Sunday 9 a.m. to Noon. (Entrance fee).*

Gozo Heritage (Son et Lumiere Museum) in Għajnsielem. *Open Monday to Saturday between 8 a.m. to 4.45 p.m. Telephone 21551475. (Entrance fee)*

Gozo 360. Citadel Cinema, Castle Hill, Victoria. *Shows last 35 minutes. Monday to Saturday 10 a.m. to 4.30 p.m. Sundays and Public Holidays, from 10.30 a.m. to 1.30 p.m. Telephone: 21559955. Monday to Saturday, Projection Times: in English, 10.30 a.m., 12.30 p.m. and 2.30 p.m. in Italian 3.30 p.m.; in French 1.30 p.m.; in German 11.30 a.m. (Telephone 21447224).*

Where to Swim

Bays and inlets in Gozo are less crowded than in Malta and some good bathing can be had at Ramla Bay (sandy), at Marsalforn, at Xlendi Bay, at Mġarr (*iż-żewwieqa*) and 'Għar

Qawqla'. More secluded are Mġarr ix-Xini, and the "inland sea" at Qawra. San Blas Bay and Daħlet Qorrot are also attractive but somewhat difficult to get to.

The Library

The Gozo Public Library is in Vajringa Street, Victoria. (Telephone 21556200)

Walking in Gozo

You can go for some pleasant walks in unspoilt Gozo and, as in Malta, the best time is between mid-October and mid-April. The areas around Annunzjata Valley (which leads to Xlendi Bay), and San Blas Valley are particularly attractive. Those who enjoy walking in the countryside and around the rugged coast should get a copy of "Countryside Walks' from the Malta Tourism Authority. Here are two suggestions:

GĦARB

Starting at the village of Għarb make your way to the Church of San Dimitri, then follow the road to Wied il-Mielaħ Valley, next to Għasri Valley. End up again at Għarb having walked past Ta' Pinu Church.

NADUR

Start off at the village of Nadur and make your way past Ta' Grejgel Valley to Daħlet Qorrot Bay; walk towards the village of Qala, have a look at the 18th century windmill and make your way back to Nadur.

Countryside Walks, published by the Tourism Authority will prove useful to those keen on walking and hiking. At the time of going to Press the following booklets were available: *Ta' Ġurdan Walk; Daħlet Qorrot Walk, The Ramla Bay Walk, The Lunzjata Walk, and The Saltpan Walk.*

Practical Information

The Gozo Hospital, Victoria. Telephone 21561600. There is also a Health Centre and Clinic in Enrico Mizzi Street, Victoria. (Tel. 21561600).

Police Station. The main Police Station is in Republic Street, Victoria (Tel. 21562040). Each town and village has its own Police Station.

Post Office. The main Post Office is also in Republic Street, Victoria (Tel. 21556435).

Tourist Information Office. Mġarr Harbour (Telephone 21553343) and in Victoria at 1 Palm Street. (Tel. 21561419).

Ministry for Gozo. Gozo has its own Ministry at St Francis Square (Pjazza San Franġisk, Victoria. (Tel. 21561482).

The Gozo Heliport. (Tel. 21557905 or 21561301). The flight takes 15 minutes and advance booking is possible through your own travel agent.

Air Malta and Air Charter Offices are at Independence Square (Pjazza Indipendenza). (Tel. 21559341/2).

Taxis are coloured white. Taxi stands are usually available at the bus terminus and at Pjazza Indipendenza in Victoria as well as at Mġarr Harbour. You can hire a car at Mġarr or Victoria. Driving is on the left with a speed limit of 64 kph on the open road and 40 kph in inhabited areas. National or International driving licences are accepted.

Transport

Apart from the bus service from Rabat to Mġarr (and vice versa) timed to coincide with the arrival and departure of the ferry boat, public transport facilities in Gozo are somewhat meagre. Self-drive cars are available in Rabat and taxis are numerous. Your taxi-driver will know every nook and cranny of Gozo and this is an advantage.

By Boat to Gozo

You can cross over to the Island of Gozo by car-ferry from Ċirkewwa (near Marfa) or from Pietà (see Map of Gozo). The trip to Mġarr in Gozo takes some 25 minutes from Ċirkewwa and around one hour and a quarter from Pietà. If you intend going to Ċirkewwa by public transport, remember that the last bus leaves the City Gate bus terminus in Valletta 75 minutes prior to the Ferry's departure. *(Check weather conditions and time-table with the Gozo Channel Company – Telephone 21556114 or 21561622 at Mġarr Gozo; and 21580435 or 21571884 at Ċirkewwa, Malta; and 21243964 for the telephone at San Maison (Pietà).*

Helicopter Service

A Malta-Gozo Helicopter service is operated by the Malta Air Charter (Telephone 22999123). The helicopter

---

Comino's most famous visitor was the Spanish Jew and mystic, Abraham ben Samuel Abulafia, who sought shelter there in 1285 hotly pursued by his enemies. He was the founder of a movement aimed at uniting Christianity, Judaism and Islam. He proclaimed himself Messiah and was expelled from Spain, Italy and Sicily.

connects the international airport in Malta to Gozo's helipad near Xewkija (Telephone 21557905). The flight takes 10 minutes.

Little Comino

Lying almost midway in the channel known as "Il-Fliegu", between Malta and Gozo, is the tiny island of Comino ("Kemmuna"). There is one hotel, 'The Comino' and should you wish to get away from the hustle and bustle of life this is the place to go to.

Rocky and arid, the Islet was once a favourite hideout for pirates, and boats crossing from Malta to Gozo were often taken by surprise by Turkish galleys. To prevent this, Grand Master Wignacourt built a Tower in 1618 and this still stands. After the building of the tower Comino became popular with the Knights of St John, who were keen on hunting the hare which was then numerous. There is also St Mary's Tower, possibly designed by architect Vittorio Cassar in 1618 to command the south Comino channel (*Il-Fliegu* – see map of Gozo on inside cover).

The small Chapel near Santa Maria Bay is said to be of great antiquity though the exact date of its erection is not known. It was visited, and condemned, by Mgr. Bueno in 1667 and re-built and re-consecrated in 1716.

A few farmers live on Comino and there is a hotel for a holiday away from it all. Comino and its inhabited neighbour Cominotto (365 metres long and 182 metres wide) afford ideal conditions for swimming.

Swimming

Particularly attractive are Santa Maria Bay, San Niklaw Bay and the "Blue Lagoon" between Comino and Cominotto. An ideal place for snorkellers, divers and windsurfers.

ISLAND OF GOZO

Comino Island

MALTA and GOZO – Sun, Sea and History

How to Get There

If staying at the Comino Hotel, their own boat will collect you from Ċirkewwa, Malta, or from the jetty on Mġarr, Gozo. Ring the Comino Hotel for details on Telephone 21529821-9.

39. Fishing nets

40. The Cathedral, said to have been built between 1697 and 1711 on a site once used as a temple to a Phoenician goddess, and (*below*) an old print of the Fungus Rock at Dwejra Bay, Gozo

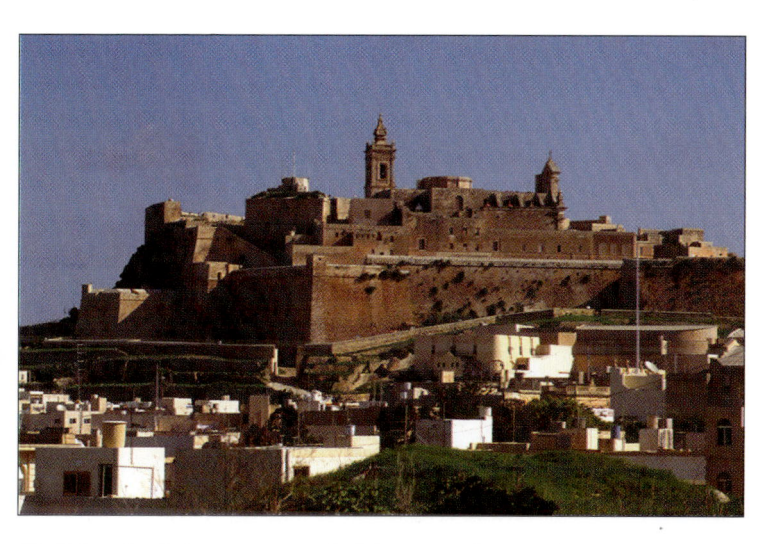

41. Victoria (Rabat), Gozo and (*below*) Ta' Pinu Basilica in the village of Għarb

42. The courtyard in the Capuchin Friary, Victoria, Gozo

43. Sandy beach at Għajn Tuffieħa Bay, Malta and (*below*) a secluded beach at Daħlet Qorrot, Gozo

44. The Blue Lagoon, Comino and (*below*) fishing boats in Marsalforn, Gozo

45. Wied il-Għasri, Gozo

46. Diving

47. Windsurfing

48. The Roman Apiary at Xemxija, St Paul's Bay and (*below*) the Chinese 'Garden of Serenity' at Santa Lucia

49. The sun sets over St Paul's Bay

Where to Stay

"All I want is a Room Somewhere"

There are over a hundred hotels in Malta, Gozo and Comino and more are being built. Their size, the prices they charge and their degree of comfort and efficiency vary considerably. Though not all are up to the desired standard, many are good or very good.

The Meridien-Phoenicia is well known and long established. There are several other five star Hotels including the Corinthia Palace, the Hilton, the Radisson, the Westin and the Inter-Continental.

The island of Gozo has 'L-Imġarr', 'Ta' Ċenċ' and the 'San Lawrenz', while the Comino Hotel on the island of that name is classified as four star.

You may already have booked your accommodation, but if you are still undecided or not satisfied with what you have got, full details of what is available can be obtained from your Travel Agent or the 'Malta Tourism Authority' (Tel. 21224444, and 21225048). For easy reference here is a short list of hotels, with their Classification which should suit most tastes and pockets.

Valletta – Floriana

Le Meridien Phoenicia. ***** Tel. 21225241. The Mall, Floriana; 136 rooms, just outside the City Gate in Valletta. Pool and Garden.

Castille.*** Castille Square, Valletta. Telephone 21243677. 39 rooms; Rooftop restaurant.

WHERE TO STAY

Sliema

Crowne Plaza.***** Tigne Street, Sliema. Telephone 21343400. 169 rooms; Pool, tennis court, sauna and gym and four restaurants. Walking distance from sea front.

Preluna Towers.**** 124 Tower Road, Sliema. Telephone 21334001. 280 rooms; Heated pool and beach facilities nearby.

Fortina.**** Tigne Sea Front, Sliema. Telephone 21343380. 193 rooms; Pool, gym and tennis court. On the waterfront.

Plevna.*** Thornton Street, Qui-Si-Sana, Sliema. Telephone 21331031. 102 rooms; Own beach facilities with pool a short walk away.

Tigne Court.*** Qui-Si-Sana, Sliema. Telephone 21332001. 87 rooms; Family hotel in residential quarter. Own beach concession.

St Julians

Hilton Malta.***** Telephone 21383383. 294 rooms; Pool and selection of restaurants.

The Westin Dragonara Resort.***** Telephone 22381000. 311 rooms; swimming pools, tennis courts. Situated in landscaped garden with the Dragonara gaming casino and The Reef Club beach Lido nearby.

Radisson Bay Point.***** Telephone 21374893. 252 rooms; swimming pools, tennis courts. Situated at the entrance to St George's Bay.

Intercontinental, Malta.***** St George's Bay, Telephone 21377600. 451 rooms, Health & Fitness Club, roof-top pool and restaurants and conference facilities.

Mdina

Xara Palace.***** Telephone 21450560. A 17th century Palazzo turned into an exclusive, beautifully furnished

Sliema & St. Julians

1. Radisson SAS Resort
2. Corinthia San Gorg Hotel
3. Corinthia Marina Hotel
4. Plaza Shopping Complex
5. Marina Hotel
6. Jesus of Nazareth Church
7. Fortina Hotel
8. Tigne Court Hotel
9. Plevna Hotel
10. Union Club
11. Casino Maltese (Club)
12. Crowne Plaza Hotel
13. Stella Maris Church
14. Preluna Hotel
15. Astra Hotel
16. Europa Hotel
17. Meadowbank/Tower Palace Hotels
18. St. James (Capua) Hospital
19. St. Patrick's Church
20. Metropole Hotel
21. St. Gregory's Church
22. Imperial Hotel
23. Church of the Sacred Heart
24. Police Station
25. HSBC Bank
26. Post Office
27. Plaza Hotel
28. Holy Trinity Church (C. of E.)
29. Carmelite Church
30. Cavalieri Hotel
31. Hilton Hotel
32. HSBC Bank
33. St. Julien Hotel
34. Westin Dragonara Hotel
35. Casino
36. Villa Rosa Hotel
37. Hotel InterContinental
38. Golden Tulip Vivaldi Hotel
39. Eden Century Cinemas
40. Bay Street Hotel Complex

.... BUS ROUTES

WHERE TO STAY

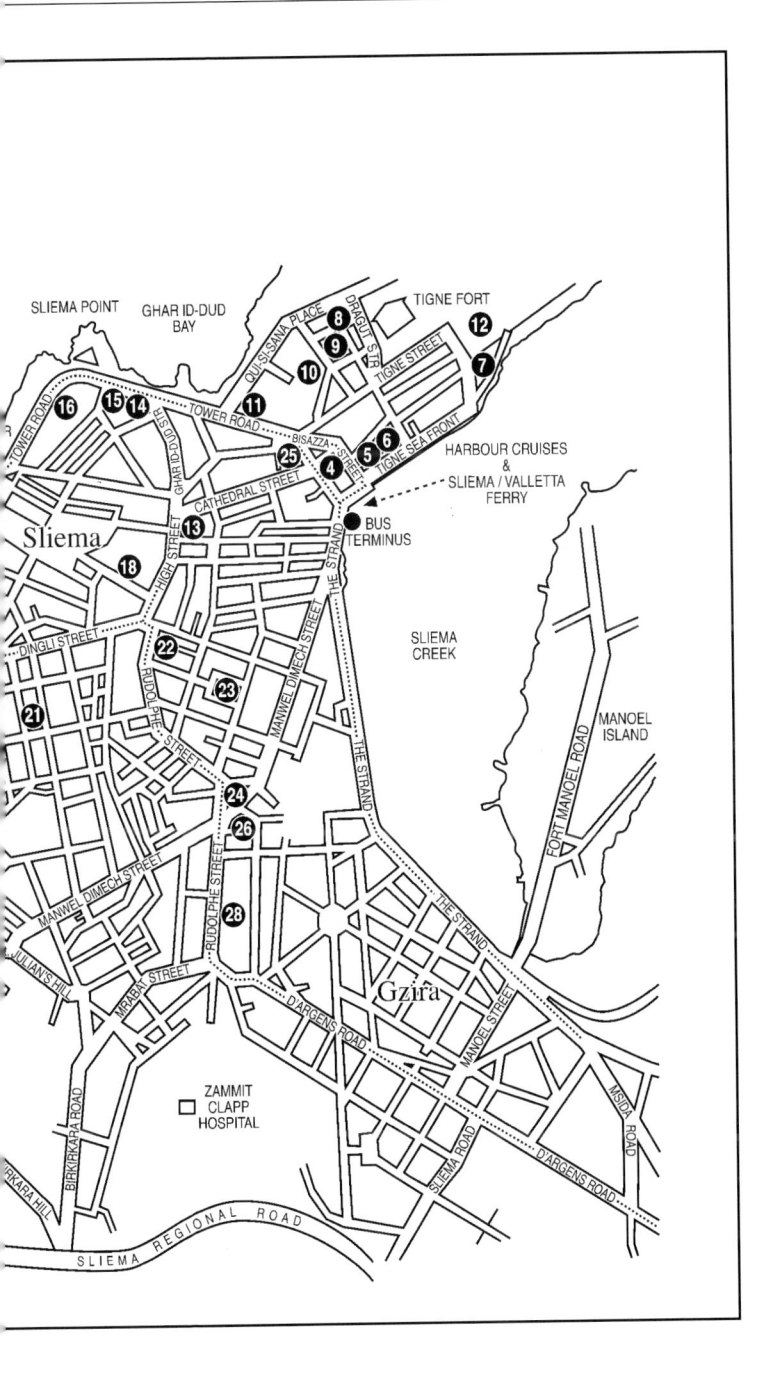

luxury hotel. Roof restaurant and a ground floor trattoria.

Attard

Corinthia Palace Hotel.***** Telephone 21440302. 155 rooms. Well appointed with heated indoor and outdoor pools, health spa and restaurants; use of San Ġorġ Lido, Corinthia Group's beach resort at St George's Bay.

Selmun, Mellieħa

Grand Hotel Mercure Selmun Palace.**** Telephone 21521040. In countryside attached to tower built by the Knights. Swimming pools, tennis. Beach nearby.

Mellieħa

Mellieħa Bay.**** Telephone 21573844. On one side of Mellieħa Bay. Pools. Watersports, tennis and gym.

Buġibba

Topaz.**** Telephone 21572416. 326 rooms and 70 timeshare apartments. Swimming pool.

Qawra

New Dolmen.**** Telephone 21581510. 386 rooms. On the coast road between Qawra and Buġibba. Pools, tennis and gym. Gaming Casino.

Grand Hotel San Antonio.**** Telephone: 21583434. 300 rooms; leisure facilities; outdoor and indoor swimming pools; health club/gym. (*Being refurbished when going to Press*)

Għajn Tuffieħa

Golden Sands. Situated above sandy beach. (New hotel being built at time of going to Press).

Marfa

Ramla Bay Resort.**** Telephone 21522181. 84 rooms. Sea front location. Pools. Private beach.

Gozo Island

L-Imġarr.***** St Anthony Street, Għajnsielem. Telephone 21560455. 20 rooms, 54 suites. Overlooking Mġarr Harbour. Pools, sauna, gym and conference facility.

Ta' Ċenċ.***** Sannat. Telephone 21556830. 64 rooms, 19 suites; swimming pools, tennis; garden; private beach (three km away).

Cornucopia.**** Triq Ġnien Imrek, Xagħra. Telephone 21556486. 50 rooms, Family hotel with five suites. Children's swimming pool, two outdoor pool.

St Patrick's.*** Xlendi. Telephone 21562951. 49 rooms some with view overlooking Xlendi Bay.

Kempinski San Lawrence Resort & Spa.*****. Telephone 21558640. Indoor and outdoor swimming pools; health club/gym; tennis courts.

Comino Island

Comino Hotel.**** Telephone 21529821. 95 rooms. Private beach; tennis courts.

Ten minutes walk away are bungalows which belong to the Hotel.

Furnished Accommodation

Many tourists prefer to rent a Villa or an apartment for their holiday abroad. These are available in Malta in increasing numbers. Prices depend on the position and facilities provided. The best way to get an apartment is through a friend's recommendation, the local Press or a Travel Agent.

Some well-appointed converted farmhouses are to be found in Gozo.

What and Where to Eat

"Meat for the Hungry, Drink for the Thirsty"

Until a few years ago the number of restaurants was few and the food, with one or two exceptions, mediocre. The reason for this is not hard to find: distances are short, most Maltese preferred to eat at home, and there was no tourist trade to speak of.

The position has changed and you can now get a first class meal at several restaurants. The food, service and ambience at restaurants such as, The Arches in Mellieħa, Mange Tout in St Paul's Bay, Lulu in St Julians, Christophers in Ta' Xbiex, The Medina in Mdina, Porto del Sol at Xemxija Hill, St Paul's Bay, Grabiel in Marsascala, the Carriage in Valletta, the Blue Room (Chinese food) in Valletta and Rubino's also in Valletta is usually very good.

Good meals in sumptuous surroundings can be had in hotels such as the Corinthia Palace, the Meridien Phoenicia, the Radisson, the Westin, the Inter Continental, Xara Palace, the Hilton, and Ta' Ċenċ in Gozo.

Food in Maltese homes is often very tasty, but so far, few restaurants specialize in Maltese dishes (apart from sea food dishes). Addresses and telephone numbers of these and other restaurants appear on pages 230-237).

Local Dishes

The cuisine in the Maltese Islands is basically English or Continental (Italian) but if you go in for local specialities here are some you might care to ask for:

Minestra: (a variant of the Italian minestrone – a thick vegetable soup; another type of Minestra, *"Kawlata"* includes beans and pork).

Braġoli: ("Beef Olives"; eggs, bacon, breadcrumbs, parsley, minced meat and olives wrapped in a thin roll of steak).

Torta tal-Lampuki: (the Lampuka is a tasty Mediterranean fish. Slices of the fish are fried and covered with pastry and then baked together with tomatoes, onions, parsley and cauliflower).

Mqarrun fil-forn: (baked macaroni with minced meat, eggs and tomato sauce).

Timpana: (baked macaroni enclosed in pastry with liver, eggs, onions, and aubergine).

Ross fil-forn: (baked rice with eggs and minced meat).

Ħut biz-zalza: (fish with caper and tomato sauce).

Qaqoċċ mimli: (stuffed globe artichokes with chopped olives, breadcrumbs and parsley).

Brunġiel fil-forn: (stuffed aubergines with minced meat, eggs, tomato sauce and grated cheese).

Ravjul: (similar to Italian ravioli served with tomato sauce and Parmesan cheese; also spaghetti, lasagne, and cannelloni).

Soppa ta' l-armla: (literally "Widows' Soup", which is a vegetable soup with poached eggs, spinach and fresh local cheese, "ġbejniet").

Fenek moqli: (fried rabbit; a favourite with many Maltese, sometimes cooked in wine).

Fish

A variety of excellent fresh fish is usually available and the best include the following: "Aċċjola", "Dentiċi", "Tunnaġ", "Ċerna", "Lampuka", "Pixxispad" (swordfish) and "Awista" (lobster).

Wine

You can buy French, Italian and German wine in practically every restaurant but if you prefer to sample the Maltese wines you will find these unpretentious and inexpensive. Among the local wines are those produced by "Marsovin" and "Delicata".

Beer

Malta beer is good. Among the favourite brands are "Hop Leaf" and "Cisk" (Lager).

Cheese

The best local cheese is the "ġbejna" which is similar to that variety of cheese known as "Chavignol" produced in central France. "Ġbejniet" are made from sheep's milk and can be dry, ("moxxi"), with or without pepper, or fresh ("frisk"). The best "ġbejna" is usually found in Gozo.

Fruit

There is a good variety of fresh fruit available, both local and imported. The best Maltese fruit are oranges (December to March) and grapes. Also delicious are strawberries, melons, mulberries, tangerines, pomegranates and figs. (Fresh fruit should be washed).

Delicious Bread

Maltese bread – fresh – is something visitors should try: most will find it delicious. (Try it with olive oil and ripe tomatoes, preferably the flat variety, 'Ħobż biż-żejt' (Bread and Olive Oil). The crusty loaf is peculiar to the Maltese islands. Several villages claim to produce the best bread; contenders include Qormi, Mellieħa, Rabat and Victoria in Gozo. In some parts of the island wood burning ovens are still in use and the bread is baked on the floor of the oven at a high temperature – this helps to give the loaf its delicious flavour. The *Ftira* – flat Maltese bread baked in a round flat disc is also excellent when served fresh from the oven.

Water

The water, though not to everyone's taste, is safe for drinking.

Restaurants (Malta)

As in the case of Hotels the quality of food, the service, the ambience and the price vary. But standards have improved in recent years and a good choice is available. For easy reference here is a list of a number of restaurants in different parts of the island and with an assorted price range. Booking is advisable.

Valletta – Floriana

Blue Room. 59 Republic Street, Valletta. Telephone 21238014. Seating 40, Chinese food. Air conditioning. ££

(The approximate cost at the time of going to press is for a meal for two including wine and service. Restaurants are classified 'First Class' to 'Fourth Class'. £ signifies inexpensive; ££ moderate; ££-£££ moderate to expensive; and £££ expensive dining. Both prices and value for money are subject to variations.)

WHAT AND WHERE TO EAT

Da Pippo Trattoria. 136 Melita Street, Valletta. Telephone 21248029. Seating 50. Air conditioning. ££

Giannini. 23 Windmill Street. Telephone 21237121. Seating 65 inside and 20 outside. Air conditioning. Vegetarian dishes if required. Open for Lunch Monday to Saturday. Parking area available. £££

Pegasus Brasserie. Floriana near City Gate. Telephone 21225241. Air conditioning. Seating 50. Area non smoking. ££-£££.

Rubino. 53 Old Bakery Street, Valletta. Telephone 21224656. Good food. Seating 48. Air conditioning. ££

The Carriage. Apartment 22, Valletta Buildings, South Street. Telephone 21247828. Seating 89 inside and outside. Closed on Sunday, Air conditioning. Vegetarian dishes if required. Lunch is served Monday to Friday. Dinner on Friday and Saturday. ££-£££.

Castille Hotel. Castille Square. Seating 80, Roof restaurant. Telephone 21243677. ££

The British Hotel. 267 St Ursola Street. Telephone 21224730. Seating 80. Some tables have an impressive view of Grand Harbour. £-££.

La Sicilia. 14 St John Street/Battery Street. Telephone 21240569. Sicilian cuisine; sitting outside gives you a striking view of Grand Harbour. £

Caffe Cordina. Telephone 21234385. In the heart of the City, Republic Street, next to the Palace Square. A favourite meeting place serving excellent confectionery. Light lunches are also served.

Sliema

Il Galeone. Telephone 21316420. Tigne Seafront. Seating 50. ££-£££.

Four Seasons. Crown Plaza Hotel, Tigne, Sliema. Telephone 21349114. Seating 180. Air conditioning. ££

T.G.I. Friday. Tower Road, Sliema. Telephone 21345897. Seating 150. ££

Hole in the Wall. Telephone 21336110. 32 High Street. Seating 75. ££

Ponte Vecchio. Tower Road. Telephone 21341591. Seating 24. ££-£££.

Magic Kiosk. St Anne Square. Telephone 21335653. Seating 120. ££

Ta' Xbiex

Christopher's Bistro. Ta' Xbiex Marina. Telephone 21337101. Seating 45. Air conditioning. ££-£££.

Manoel Island

Royal Malta Yacht Club. Telephone 21313291. Indoors and outdoors (facing the sea). Italian chef, closed on Monday and Sunday evening. ££

St Julians

Barracuda. Telephone 21331817. 194 Main Street. Seating 95. Vegetarian dishes if required. ££-£££.

Bottega del Vino at the Hilton, Portomaso. Telephone 21383383. Seating 72. Air conditioning. Area for non-smoking. £££

The Blue Elephant also at Hilton. Telephone 21383383. Thai food. Seating 160 inside and 50 outside. Air conditioning. £££

Davidoff's at the Radisson SAS Bay Point Resort St George's Bay. Telephone 21374894. Seating 60. Air conditioning. £££

Girasole, Spinola Bay. Telephone 21332000. Overlooking Spinola Bay. Good food. Seating 90 ££.

La Dolce Vita. 159 St George's Road. Telephone 21337806. Seating 200. Overlooking Spinola Bay. ££-£££.

Lulu. 30 Church Street. Telephone 21377211. Seating 40. Air conditioning. Vegetarian dishes if required. ££-£££.

Peppino's Restaurant. 30 St George's Road, St Julians. Telephone 21373200. Seating 60 inside and 30 outside. Overlooking Spinola Bay. Air conditioning. ££-£££

San Giuliano. Spinola Bay. Telephone 21332000. Seating 90. Overlooking Spinola Bay. Vegetarian dishes if required. £££

Caffe Raffael. Spinola Road. Telephone 21319988. Bayside location £-££.

Pulcinella. St George's Road. Telephone 21359865. Pizzeria. £

Marsascala

Grabiel. Mifsud Bonnici Square. Telephone 21634194. Seating 65. Air conditioning. Vegetarian dishes if required. Fresh fish. Closed on Sunday. ££-£££.

Il Re Del Pesce. Triq id-Daħla ta' San Tumas. Telephone 21636353. Seating 90 inside and 90 outside. Air conditioning. Vegetarian dishes if required. Fresh fish. Closed most Sundays. ££-£££.

St Paul's Bay

Mange Tout. 356, St Paul's Street, Xemxija, St Paul's Bay. Telephone 21572121. Seating 32. Air conditioning. Vegetarian dishes if requested. Good parking facilities. £££

Da Rosi Restaurant. 44 Church Street. Telephone 21571411. Air conditioning. Vegetarian dishes if required. ££

Gillieru. Church Street. Telephone 21573480. Seating 180 inside and 299 outside. Air conditioning. Vegetarian dishes if required. Fresh fish. On the water's edge. ££

Mistra Tourist Village. Xemxija Hill, Xemxija, St Paul's Bay. Telephone 21580481. ££.

Porto del Sol. Xemxija Hill. Telephone 21573970. Seating 60. Air conditioning. Good view of bay. Vegetarian dishes if required. Closed on Sunday. ££-£££

Mellieħa

The Arches. G. Borg Olivier Street. Telephone 21523460. Seating 100. Vegetarian dishes if required. Closed on Sunday. £££

The Great Dane and Dynasty Restaurant (Danish Village) at the Mellieħa Holiday Centre. Telephone 21572460. ££

Mdina

The Medina. Holy Cross Street. Telephone 21454004. Seating 100 inside and 50 outside. Opening hours 7.30 to 10.30 p.m. Closed on Sunday. Vegetarian dishes if required. £££

Bacchus. Inguanez Street. Telephone 21454981. Seating 650 inside and 500 outside. ££

Xara Palace Hotel. Misraħ il-Kunsill. Telephone 21450560. Seating 60 inside and 30 outside. Open 7.30 p.m. Air conditioning. Spectacular view from the open air terrace. Vegetarian dishes if required. £££

The Trattoria. AD 1530. Misraħ il-Kunsill. Telephone 21450560. Seating 60 inside and 50 outside. £-££.

Ciapetti. St Agatha's Esplanade. Telephone 21459987. Seating 80. £-££

Città Vecchia. Bastion Square, with panoramic view. Telephone 21454511. £
Palazzo Notabile. Villegaignon Street. Telephone 21454625. £-££
Fontanella. Tea Rooms. Bastion Street. Telephone 21450208.

Rabat

Il-Veduta. Saqqajja Square. Telephone 21454666. Seating 180 inside and 180 outside. Next to Mdina's Main gate. Air conditioning. £-££
The Grapes. St Agatha Street. Telephone 21450483. Seating 80. £
Rogantino's. Il-Palazz l-Aħmar, Wied il-Busbies, Landrijiet (L/o Rabat) Telephone 21452003. (*Booking Advisable*) ££

Dingli

Bobbyland. Dingli Cliffs. Telephone 21452895. Seating 80 outside and 50 inside. Air conditioning. Panoramic view. ££

Mosta

The Lord Nelson. Triq il-Kbira. Telephone 21432590. Seating 55. Closed on Sunday and Monday. Air conditioning. Vegetarian dishes if required. £££
Ta' Marija. Constitution Street. Telephone 21434444, (Maltese food) Seating 50. ££

Balzan

Corinthia Restaurant. Corinthia Palace Hotel. De Paule Avenue, San Anton, Balzan. Telephone 21440302.

Village of Marsaxlokk

Seating 280. Air conditioning. Vegetarian dishes if requested. Non smoking area. £££

Marsaxlokk

Hunters Tower. Wilga Street, Marsaxlokk. Telephone 21651792. Seating 75. ££

Marsascala

La Favorita. Gardell Street. Telephone 21634113. ££

Gozo and Comino

Victoria – Rabat

Il-Panzier. Charity Street. Telephone 21559979 (Closed on Monday) £££

Mġarr

Il-Kċina tal-Barrakka. Manuel de Vilhena Street. Telephone 21556543. ££ Open in Summer and booking advisable.

Marsalforn

Ta' Frenċ. Marsalforn Road. Telephone 21553888. Dinner only. ££
Il-Kartell. Triq il-Forn. Telephone 21556918. Good fish. £-££

Għarb

Jeffrey's. Triq il-Għarb. Telephone 21561006. Dinner only. Closed on Sunday. Booking advisable. ££
Otter's. Triq Santa Marija. Telephone 21562473. Good fish, salad. Sea front. £

Xagħra

Oleander. Piazza Vittoria. Telephone 21557230. Local dishes. £-££
Gesther. Vjal it-8 ta' Settembru. Telephone 21556621. £-££

Xlendi

Paradise. Triq il-Madonna tal-Karmnu. Telephone 21556878. Simple cooking. Closed Monday. £

Entertainment

Theatre

The island's national Theatre is the Manoel Theatre at 115 Old Theatre Street, Valletta. (Tel. 21246389). Opening hours: Monday to Friday, 10 a.m. to 1 p.m. and 5 p.m. to 7 p.m.; Saturday 10 a.m. to noon. (Reservations Telephone 21246389).

Opera, concerts, plays and ballet are held between October and May.

A visit to the Manoel Theatre is free and tours are generally held Monday to Friday 10.45 a.m. and 11.30 a.m., Saturday 11.30 a.m., and include a visit to the Theatre's small Museum (open Monday to Friday, 10 a.m. to 1 p.m., 3 p.m. to 6 p.m. Free concerts are also given in the theatre's recital room every Wednesday at 12.30 p.m.)

Concerts are sometimes also held at the Mediterranean Conference Centre, in Mediterranean Street, Valletta. Telephone 21243840.

The Bay Street Entertainment Complex, is at St Georges Bay, St Julians. (Tel. 21380600).

Ice Ring

The Eden Ice Arena, is at St Georges Bay, St Julians. Telephone 23710100.

Gambling

The people of Malta enjoy a flutter and various lotteries are held on a weekly basis. The National Lottery is held four times a year.

There are three gambling casinos, the Dragonara Palace Casino in St Julians, the Oracle at the New Dolmen Hotel, Buġibba, and the Casino di Venezia in Vittoriosa. International rules apply to roulette, Black Jack and *Chemin de fer*. All three Casinos have restaurants. Passports or Identity Cards must be produced on a first visit. Minimum age of entry is 18.

Dragonara Palace Casino

St Julians. Telephone 21382362.

The Oracle Casino

New Dolmen Hotel, Buġibba. Telephone 21570057.

Casino di Venezia

Vittoriosa. Telephone 21805581.

Cinema

There are some thirty screens in Malta and two in Gozo. The biggest complex, Eden Century is at George's Bay, St Julians. (Tel. 21376408 and 21376117). There are also Cinema complexes at Fgura, (Tel. 21808000) and Marsascala and at the Embassy Cinema in Valletta (Tel. 21222225) and in Victoria, Gozo (Tel. 21559955). Check with the Newspapers for details.

Television

A wide cross section of Television stations can be picked up in Malta and Gozo. Cable Television provides some fifty channels including BBC World, BBC Prime, Granada UKTV, National Geographic, SKY, CNN, Eurosport, Animal Planet, Biography Channel, Travel, Children's Cartoon Network, Muzzik, the Movie Channel and MGM Movies among others. Most Italian channels are available including RAI Uno, Due, Tre, Canale 5, Italia 1 and Rete 4. A channel in German (Deutche Welle), one in French, one in Spanish and one in Arabic are also provided.

Disco – Nightclubs

Nightlife in Malta revolves for the most part around Paceville and St Julians with several disco-nightclubs which are to be found in St George's Road and St George's Bay, both in Paceville.

Audio Visual Shows:

The Malta Experience

Two parts of the Mediterranean Conference Centre in Valletta (The former *Sacra Infermeria*, hospital of the Knights) is used for showing 'The Malta Experience', a dramatic audio visual of the main events in the islands chequered history. Show every hour Monday to Friday 11 a.m. to 4 p.m.; Saturday and Sunday 11 a.m. to 1 p.m. *Entrance fee.*

ENTERTAINMENT

The Knights Hospitallers

The other exhibition area is devoted to the 'Knights Hospitallers' open Monday to Friday 9.30 a.m. to 4 p.m.; Saturday and Sunday 9.30 a.m. to 1 p.m. and consists of tableaux showing activities of the Knights. *Entrance fee.*

The Great Siege

'The Great Siege of Malta and The Knights of St John', a 45-minute re-enactment of the history of the Order of St John in Malta, Open daily Monday to Sunday. From 9 a.m. to last admission at 4 p.m. At the Cafè Premier Complex, Republic Street, Valletta. (Tel. 21247300). *Entrance fee.*

The Wartime Experience

The 'Wartime Experience' is a powerful audio-visual show using much actual newsreel footage of the island's decisive stand during World War II. The show alternates with another called 'The Valletta Experience', Embassy Cinema Complex St Lucia Street, Valletta. *Entrance fee.* (Tel. 21227436 and 21245818).

Sacred Island

A multi-media show. A journey through time – the culture and folklore of the Maltese people. Produced by the Religious Tourism Organization, at *Dar l-Emigranti*, Upper Barrakka, Valletta. Weekday at 10 a.m., 11.30, 1 p.m., 2.30 p.m. and 4 p.m.; Saturday 10 a.m., 11.30, and 1 p.m. Sundays and Public Holidays 10 a.m., 11.30 a.m. *Entrance fee.*

The Mdina Experience

A multimedia show highlighting the history of the old City. Open daily Monday to Friday 10.30 a.m. to 4 p.m. Saturday 10.30 a.m. to 2 p.m. Mesquita Square, Mdina. (Tel. 21454322 and 21450055). (*Entrance fee*).

Tales of a Silent City

Palazzo Gatto Murina, Villegaignon Street, Mdina. A multimedia show with commentary available in English as well as Italian. German and French. (Tel. 214511179 and 21451834). (*Entrance fee*).

Keeping Children Amused

A sandy beach usually keeps children occupied and amused. Try Mellieħa Bay, Golden Bay, Għajn Tuffieħa Bay, Paradise Bay, Ġnejna Bay in Malta and Ramla Bay in Gozo. (see Maps and Plans, Bus Routes and Taxis).

Most of the large hotels provide for the needs of children. This is specially true of Mistra Village a self-catering 'tourist village', ideal for families with a host of facilities available. Xemxija Hill, St Paul's Bay. (Tel. 21580481). Buses 43, 44, 45, 50.

The White Rocks, in the North of the Island, is home to 'Splash & Fun Waterpark', Mediterraneo Marine World. Baħar Iċ-Ċagħaq. Telephone 21372218. (Bus No 68 from Valletta, and Bus No 70 from Buġibba).

Other family attractions include Popeye Village, at Anchor Bay, Mellieħa, (Telephone 21570579); and the Bay Street Complex in St George's Bay. (Telephone 21380600).

Horse Riding. Friendly stables at Golden Bay, Għajn Tuffieħa. All standards of riding (Tel. 21573360). Also at Marsa.

ENTERTAINMENT

Playmobil Funpark

The Playmobil Funpark is at B36 Bulebel Industrial Estate in Żejtun (Tel. 21693764). Opening hours: October to June, Monday to Friday 9 a.m. to 6 p.m. Saturday and Sunday 3 p.m. to 6 p.m.; July to September, Monday to Friday, 9 a.m. to 6 p.m., Saturday 6 p.m. to 9 p.m.; Sunday closed. (Bus 29) (Planning to move to Ħal Far at the time of going to Press).

The Toy Museum

The Toy Museum at 222 Republic Street will amuse both adults and children. Situated opposite Casa Rocca Piccolo (see page 59). The opening hours are Monday to Friday 10.30 a.m. to 3.30 p.m.; Saturday and Sunday 10.30 to 1.30 p.m. (*Entrance fee, through accompanied children are allowed in free of charge*).

Traditions and Crafts of Malta

Traditions and Crafts of Malta will also interest both children and adults. A commentary in English and other languages is available. Situated at St John Cavalier, which formed part of the defence of Valletta, (next to the Embassy of the Order of St John). It is open Monday to Sunday (including Public Holidays) between 10 a.m. to 5.30 p.m. Closed on Saturday. A cafeteria is available. (*Entrance fee*).

Shooting Films

The large water tank at Rinella attracts film producers to the island, and among cinema films shot or partly shot in Malta were the latest version of 'The Count of Monte Cristo', 'Swept Away' (Ritchie-Madonna), 'Cutthroat Island', 'Killer Whale', 'Raise the Titanic' and 'U-571'.

A Note on Shopping

"To serve us seems their only aim"

There are many shops in Malta – good, bad and indifferent – and it is not the purpose of this guide book to list or evaluate them. But a few tips on where to find the better shopping centres and what to look for will come in handy.

As indicated elsewhere, most shops open between 9 a.m. and 7 p.m. with two or three hours break for lunch. Shops may remain open until 10 p.m. on Thursday, Friday and Saturday. Most shops are closed on Sunday and Public Holidays (see page 285) but some remain open on these days.

Pharmacies open at 8.30 until 1 p.m. and from 3 p.m. until 8 p.m. On Sundays one Pharmacy remains open in each town and village from 9 a.m. to 12.30 p.m. (A list of these is published in the *Sunday Times of Malta* and the *Independent on Sunday*). Jewellers and shops selling jewellery and silver close at 1 p.m. on Saturday.

Shopping Centres

The main shopping centres in Valletta are in Republic Street, Merchants Street, Old Bakery Street, St Lucia Street and Melita Street, and in Sliema these are to be found around the Strand and Tower Road (next to the Strand) and Manuel Dimech Street. Some good shops are also to be found in St Julians, Birkirkara, and in Ħamrun.

A NOTE ON SHOPPING

Things to Look For

Tastes vary considerably and it is difficult to advise on what to buy. But the following are good value and most of them will be appreciated as having been made in the Maltese islands.

Attractive choice of Maltese ceramics at Ceramica Saracina at 77/78 St Anthony's Street, Attard, Malta, (Tel. 21417973). Open Tuesday and Thursday 8.30 a.m. to 5 p.m.

Artistic stone sculpture from Neolithic Malta at 'Ta' Peppi' Baħħara Street, Għajnsielem, Gozo. (Tel. 21553559).

Original oil paintings and watercolours by a Maltese artist (Marco Cremona) are available at the 'Galleria Cremona' at 16 Museum Road, Rabat. (Tel. 21450509) and in Mesquita Square, Mdina.

A substantial number of second hand books, including books on Malta, can be found at 'Island Books (Liz Groves) 4/1 St Anthony Street, Mosta. Open Saturdays, Sundays and Public Holidays 8.30 a.m. to 5 p.m. (Tel. 21432774).

A fine variety of fine China – Meissen, Dresden, Wedgwood, Sevres, Waterford, Minton, and others are to be found at Gio. Batta Delia in Republic Street (opposite the ruined Opera House in Valletta). (Tel. 21233618). Closed on Sunday.

Antique engravings, maps and paintings are on sale at 'Collectors' Den' in Archbishop Street, Valletta (Tel. 21231845).

Watercolours of Maltese scenes at C. Galea Paintings, at 8 Merchants Street, Valletta (Tel. 21243591); and at Galea's Studio, South Street, Valletta (Tel.21237455).

Malta weave can be found at 'Weaving and Lace Craft' 25 Saqqajja Square, Rabat. (Tel. 21454436).

How about some capers, cheeslets (*Ġbejna*) and olives to take back home?

Other recommended items include

Malta Glass (at Ta' Qali) and Gozo Glass in Għarb, Gozo
Hand-made lace, (including mantillas and table-cloths).
Silverware (959, 917, 875 and 800 millims, marked with a Maltese Cross).
Gold (including links, brooches and ear-rings; marked with a crown if 22 or 18 carat and with a shield if 9, 12, or 15 carat).
Filigree (gold and silver) and including brooches and bracelets).
Articles made of wrought iron, "ferrobattuto" (small tables, candlesticks etc.).
Pottery.
Maltese dolls wearing the traditional "faldetta" or in country costume.
Ceramics, including glazed tiles depicting local scenes.
Crochet, shawls and jackets.
Malta Stamps.
Old Prints and Maps of Malta.
Antiques.

If you want to be different you can go in for a pair of brass dolphin door-knockers, a dozen or two Malta oranges or even a Maltese Wall Clock (see page 274), or you can buy copies of this guide book for your friends back home!

Useful to note the following

Malta Government Crafts Centre, St John's Square, Valletta (Tel. 21221221);
Ta' Qali Crafts Village, Ta' Qali, Malta;
Fontanella Crafts Village, La Fontana, Xlendi-Victoria Road, Gozo; and
Ta' Dbiegi Crafts Village, Limits of St Lawrenz, Gozo (Tel. 21556202).

Open Air Markets

Valletta. A market takes place every day in Merchants Street, and on a Sunday the market is held just outside the City Gate in St James's Ditch.

Open-air markets are held in Rabat on a Sunday morning, in Cospicua on a Tuesday morning; in Marsaxlokk, mornings with fresh fish on sale on a Sunday.

In Gozo the open market is held in the main Square, it-Tokk, in Victoria.

Chemists

The Pharmacy at the International Airport is open Monday to Sunday from 9 a.m. to 8 p.m.

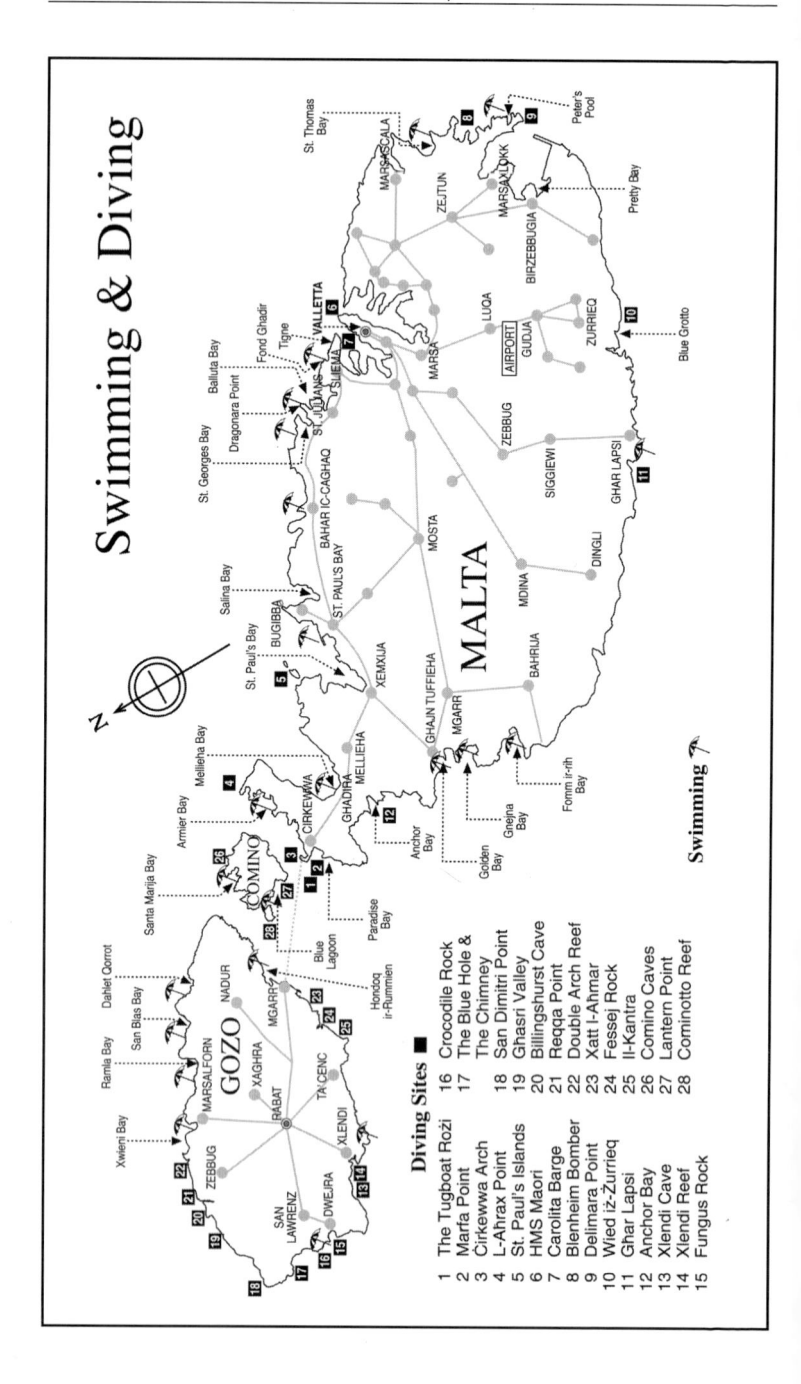

MALTA and GOZO – Sun, Sea and History

Swimming & Diving

Diving Sites ■

1. The Tugboat Rozi
2. Marfa Point
3. Cirkewwa Arch
4. L-Ahrax Point
5. St. Paul's Islands
6. HMS Maori
7. Carolita Barge
8. Blenheim Bomber
9. Delimara Point
10. Wied iż-Żurrieq
11. Ghar Lapsi
12. Anchor Bay
13. Xlendi Cave
14. Xlendi Reef
15. Fungus Rock
16. Crocodile Rock
17. The Blue Hole & The Chimney
18. San Dimitri Point
19. Ghasri Valley
20. Billingshurst Cave
21. Reqqa Point
22. Double Arch Reef
23. Xatt l-Ahmar
24. Fessej Rock
25. Il-Kantra
26. Comino Caves
27. Lantern Point
28. Cominotto Reef

Swimming

248

Swimming and other Sports

Swimming

When you've done the sights (or even before) and had your fill of prehistoric temples, medieval palaces and baroque churches, it is time to relax, bask in the sun and have a swim. You can do this any time between May and October, and the hardy ones add April and November for good measure.

Bathing is safe practically anywhere in Malta and Gozo and is quite delightful around Comino. There are no tides and few treacherous currents[1]. The sea temperature averages 74°F. (22.7C). between May and October. You can be sure of an average 6.4 hours of daily sunshine in winter, and 10.6 hours in summer.

Those who are meticulous and want details of daily hours of sunshine and temperature and of the rainfall month by month, are referred to page 256. For the rest, its enough to say that the sea is never far away and you can have a gorgeous suntan in no time at all. Indeed if you are here in July or August it is best to tan in easy stages, especially if you are not used to the hot sun, or are blonde or a red head beauty.

Efforts are being taken to keep the beaches clean – you can play your part by using the litter bins.

---

[1] But avoid bathing at Għajn Tuffieħa Bay if a Red Flag is displayed.

Għajn Tuffieħa Bay

Where to Swim

If you prefer sand to rock there are small and attractive beaches in the north of the Island, all of which are sandy or partly sandy including Golden Bay, Għajn Tuffieħa Bay, Ġnejna Bay, Mellieħa Bay, Armier Bay, Anchor Bay and Paradise Bay; (see map on page 248).

Although you can get to or near to most of these by bus (City Gate Terminus, bus, No. 43) it is best to go there by car. Another small, partly sandy beach is at St George's Bay, St Julians.

Off the Rocks

If you prefer bathing off-the-rocks you can do so practically anywhere along the coast stretching from Tigne (Sliema) to Dragonara (St Julians). Along the sea-front you can swim

SWIMMING AND OTHER SPORTS

at Qui-si-Sana, Għar id-Dud, Fond Għadir, the Exiles, Balluta Bay and Dragonara (see map). Sliema is the most modern town in Malta and is within easy reach of Valletta – less than four miles away. (see Bus Routes on page 281).

Other good spots for swimming can be found at Peter's Pool, Marsascala, St Paul's Bay, Baħar Iċ-Ċagħaq, Għar Lapsi, Wied Iż-Żurrieq and St Thomas Bay. (Here again it is best to go by car).

Most of these swimming resorts and especially the sandy beaches are crowded on weekends and Public Holidays. They are less crowded on weekdays during the morning.

The Reef Club

The Reef Club at Dragonara is one of the best available, and the Corinthia Resort at St George's is also a favourite. Please remember that nude sunbathing is not permitted.

Other Sports

Diving

Malta is a diver's paradise. (See map on page 248) which lists twenty-eight popular Dive Sites.

If you go in for diving, water skiing, aqua-planing, sailing, snorkel fishing and boating (or if you want to learn) Malta is good place for it.

Golf

A Golf course is located at Marsa Sports Club (Tel. 21233851). Non-members welcome, and clubs can be rented. Squash can also be played here.

Windsurfing

Windsurfing is available at many of the major beaches since this is a well established sport.

Sailing and Yachting

Sailing regattas are held regularly between April and November. The Valletta Yacht Club at Manoel Island (Tel. 21333109) is available for giving information about yacht charter.

Horse Riding

There are several riding schools near Golden Bay and in the area near the Marsa race track.

Races are held every Sunday between October and May.

Bowling

Eden Super Bowl in St Augustine Street, Paceville (Tel. 21387398).

Rock Climbing

Rock climbing is another sport which is becoming popular in Malta. If you are fit, you may wish to try climbing in the following areas:

The Victoria Lines; Fomm ir-Riħ Bay; Għar Lapsi; the Blue Grotto; Wied Babu (near the Blue Grotto); Wied il-Qirda; and in Gozo you could try climbing at the Inland Sea; Wardija point and Mġarr ix-Xini.

Harbour Cruises

Tour of the Harbours

Vessels berthed at the Strand, Sliema, take you on tours of the Island's harbours and historical battlements. Usual time of departure: 10.30 a.m. and 3.30 p.m. Other vessels, also at the Strand, take you to Comino and Gozo. Usual time of departure: 9 a.m.

Marsamxett Harbour

Your tour starts at the Strand in Sliema and turns south across Sliema Creek towards Manoel Island. The boat takes you past Manoel Island and Fort Manoel, (now being developed as a tourist complex). The Fort was erected at the expense of Grand Master Manoel de Vilhena, a Portuguese who ruled between 1722 and 1736.

An isolation hospital to deal with cases of the dreaded plague which was prevalent in medieval times was built on Manoel Island. Many interesting people passed through this hospital, known as the Lazzaretto, including Disraeli in 1830, Sir Walter Scott a year later, Thackeray in 1844, the Rev (later Cardinal) Newman in 1852 and Lord Byron on his second visit in 1811.

In World War II the Lazzaretto was used as a submarine base.

During your cruise of the Harbour you will notice the Yacht Marina, Sa Maison Gardens, Hastings Gardens, St

Paul's Anglican pro-Cathedral, and the Auberge d'Angleterre and de Baviere, which served as headquarters for the Anglo-Bavarian Langue of the Order of St John in 1784. Finally, Fort St Elmo, which bore the brunt of the Turkish attacks during the Great Siege of 1565.

Grand Harbour

You go next to Grand Harbour; described by some as the finest in the world. Landmarks which you will see include the Mediterranean Conference Centre (formerly the Hospital of the Order); the Lower Barracca, a public Garden; the Church of Our Lady of Liesse, first built in 1620 and re-built in 1740 at the expense of the Langue of France; the Upper Barracca Gardens, and the Saluting Battery, dating back to 1661.

Other places to note are the Sir Paul Boffa Hospital, the Dockyard, and Senglea, Cospicua and Vittoriosa and of course Fort St Angelo proudly in command of the great harbour, perhaps the most famous Fort in Malta. Fort Ricasoli commands a strategic position at the entrance to Grand Harbour. Finally, Fort Tigne (1792) before returning to the Strand in Sliema.

Mediterranean Climate

"Every Sky has its Beauty"

Malta's climate is Mediterranean. This means it is warm and can get very hot; cool but rarely cold.

The hottest months are July and August (average 78°F-25.6°C) and the coolest January and February (average 55°F – 12.8°C. The temperature rarely falls below 50°F (except at night), but it does get cold indoors if your room is not properly heated. March tends to be blowy and unpredictable and September humid.

All in all however, the climate is good with plenty of sunshine, as you can see from the chart on the next page.

The main characteristics of the Maltese climate have been concisely summed up as "summer drought, mild winters with, for a large part of the year, clear blue skies and a high light intensity".

As suggested on page 28, warm clothing is recommended for December to February, lighter wear from March to May and during October and November, and very light clothing between June and September. A raincoat may be useful between October and March.

The heat of Summer is often tempered by cool breezes from the north which makes it pleasant; occasionally a hot and humid south easterly wind known locally as the *Xlokk* makes things unpleasant, but fortunately this is not a too frequent occurance. It was this wind which so upset Byron (see page 39). A different view of the Island's climate was taken by Thomas McGill who, in dedicating his guide-book to Queen Adelaide in 1838 wrote (of the area around the

	Sunshine	Average Temperature				Rainfall	
Month	Hours*	Max.		Min.		Ins.	mm.
January	5.2	63°F	17.2°C	46°F	7.8°C	3.26	83.5
February	5.1	64°F	17.8°C	47°F	8.3°C	2.17	55.6
March	6.9	68°F	20.0°C	48°F	8.9°C	1.58	40.5
April	8.5	72°F	22.2°C	51°F	10.6°C	0.87	22.3
May	10.2	78°F	25.6°C	50°F	13.3°C	0.41	10.5
June	11.7	85°F	29.4°C	63°F	17.2°C	0.08	2.0
July	12.6	92°F	33.3°C	69°F	20.6°C	0.02	0.5
August	11.9	91°F	32.8°C	70°F	21.1°C	0.22	5.6
September	9.1	86°F	30.0°C	69°F	20.6°C	1.19	30.5
October	7.1	82°F	27.8°C	63°F	17.2°C	3.25	83.3
November	5.9	74°F	23.3°C	54°F	12.2°C	3.39	86.9
December	5.1	67°F	19.4°C	49°F	9.4°C	3.81	97.7

* This represents cloudless sunshine and not the time from sunrise to sunset.

village of Qrendi): "The fine air on all this portion of the Island is truly exhilarating, and would put even a cynic in jovial humour".

Summer usually breaks in September to be followed, in mid-October to mid-November, by an Indian summer known locally as St Martin's summer. Despite heavy downpours which sometimes occur during these months, many find this period the most pleasant of the year.

Because of its exposed position, the winds are important and buildings are often sited to avoid them. In an interesting footnote in his book "The Buildings of Malta 1530-1795", Quentin Hughes records the following statistics:

"The winter tramontana (north wind) blows 6% of the year and often carries hail; the scirocco for 13% in Spring and Autumn

blows from the south-east, sand-laden from the African desert, it picks up moisture from the sea. The gregale (15%) is a violent blistery wind which usually blows for a period of three days and then ceases as rapidly as it came: it blows from the north-east; and the pleasant cool breezes of the mistral, which are so welcome in summer (29%) blow over the sea from the north-west."

Weather Lore

Those who are skeptical of statistics and weather reports, may wish to put their faith in Maltese weather lore. Many of the following items were collected and published by Fr. Manuel Magri in 1902:

1. On Candlemas Day (February 2) the bear comes out of his cave. If he finds his paws wet, winter is finished; if they are dry, winter is still to come.
2. The eve and day of St Lawrence (August 9 and 10) are said to have the hottest and most burning sun of the whole year.
3. On the Feast of the Assumption (August 15) the weather changes and becomes cooler. Clouds appear and are known as *Gharixa ta' Santa Marija*, "St Mary's shelter". *Gharix* means a shelter built in a field to protect workman from the sun during their noon rest period.
4. On St Bartholomew's day (August 24) the first rain is due. St Bartholomew was given the keys to the skies and when black clouds appear the Saint is said to be oiling his keys.
5. St Martin's Summer. (Second week-end of November). The crops rejoice in it.
6. By St Andrew's Day (November 30)
   Half the barns are filled for the year,
   Half the sowing is done,
7. Before Christmas
   It is never cold nor chilly

8. If the sky is covered with lambs' wool clouds there will be rain or violent wind.
9. Evening glow,
   Get the mare ready for the races.
10. Morning glow,
    feed your cows and keep them in.

Points of the Compass

Finally, the points of the compass in Maltese; these may come in useful if you are planning to sail, swim or walk and wish to ask for a forecast of wind direction: North: *Tramuntana*; North East: *Grigal* (this is the one which shipwrecked St Paul in Malta in A.D. 60); East: *Lvant*; South-East: *Xlokk* (this is the unpleasant one); South: *Nofs-in-Nhar*; South West: *Lbic*; West: *Punent*; North West: *Majjistral*. Briefly, north and west winds are cool; east and south winds are hot; south-west and north east are in between.

Half-Day Excursions

"'Doing' the Sights"

Many visitors only have a short time at their disposal and will be able to do and see only some of the things listed in this guide book. Here are some suggestions for excursions for those in a hurry.

1. Valletta. Visit St John's Co-Cathedral and the Cathedral Museum; the Grand Master's Palace and the Palace Armoury; and end up at the Upper Barrakka Gardens overlooking the Grand Harbour.
2. Valletta. Visit the Museum of Archaeology or the Museum of Fine Arts; the Bibliotheca; the Manoel Theatre; walk down Old Bakery Street to St Elmo and then on to Irish Street and the Lower Barracca Gardens.
3. Mdina. The old Capital City.
4. San Anton Gardens; Mosta Dome, Wardija and drive along the Coast Road to Sliema, stopping at the Kennedy Grove at Salina.
5. Hypogeum; Tarxien Neolithic Temples; Għar Dalam and the fishing village of Marsaxlokk.
6. Prehistoric temples of Ħaġar Qim and Mnajdra: Wied iż-Żurrieq, and by boat to the Blue Grotto.
7. Buskett Gardens; Dingli Cliffs; and St Paul's Catacombs in Rabat.
8. Countryside. (October to April), Baħrija and Mtaħleb with a look at Mdina on your way back.
9. Whole day excursion to the Island of Gozo.

Licensed Guides

Qualified guides are available through the Malta Tourism Authority (Tel. 21224444).

Hints for the Motorist

"Like the Driving of Jehu"

It must be said that though there are many pleasant things to do in Malta, motoring is not high on the list. Distances tend to be short, streets, especially secondary ones, narrow and the general standards of driving not all they should be. The state of some roads leaves much to be desired.

A small car is recommended, and you will find that due to frequent gear-changing few cars perform the mileage to the gallon which is claimed. Parking is another consideration.

You will need a British or international driving licence and an endorsement from the Police Headquarters in Floriana. If you are driving your own car no endorsement is necessary. Keep the following points in mind.

1. If you hire a car make sure it is comprehensively insured.
2. Driving is on the LEFT and driving signs are in English.
3. If at all possible avoid driving behind a bus, lorry or truck.
4. On a wet day drive carefully on a lower gear.
5. Parking can be a problem in Valletta especially if you get in after 9 a.m. Car Park Attendants are usually given a 20-25 cents tip.
6. Pedestrians expect you to use your horn.
7. A special licence is needed to enter Valletta, and, if not a resident of Mdina, a permit is needed to enter the City.

8. Signal clearly and early – do not expect everyone else to do likewise.
9. The official speed limit is 40 kph (23 mph), in built-up areas and 60 kph (40 mph) in open country.
10. Seat belts are compulsory.
11. Overtake on the right. (Overtaking on the left is not uncommon!).
12. Always expect the unexpected.

Approximate Distances from Valletta

	Miles	Kms.
Attard	4	6.50
Buskett	8	12.85
Delimara	8	12.85
Dingli Cliffs	8½	13.50
Ħasan's Cave	9	14.50
Malta International Airport, Gudja	4	6.50
Marfa & Ċirkewwa	16	25.75
Marsaxlokk	6	9.60
Mellieħa	13	21.00
Mdina	7	11.25
Mosta	5½	9.00
St Paul's Bay	9½	15.25
San Anton Gardens	4	6.50
St Julians	5	8.00
Sliema	4	6.50
Żurrieq (Blue Grotto)	6	9.60
Rabat	7	11.25

Distances from Victoria (Gozo)

	Miles	Kms.
Calypso's Cave	4	6.50
Daħlet Qorrot Bay	5	8.00
Dwejra Bay	3½	5.70
Ġgantija Temples	2½	4.00
Marsalforn Bay	2	3.25
Qala	4	6.50
Ramla Bay (via Nadur)	7	11.25
(via Xagħra)	5½	8.85
Xlendi Bay	2	3.25

Distances from Mġarr (Gozo)

Victoria (Rabat)	4	6.50
Calypso's Cave	5	8.00
Daħlet Qorrot Bay	3	4.80
Dwejra Bay	7½	12.00
Ġgantija Temples	4	6.50
Qala	1½	2.50
Marsalforn Bay	6	9.60
Ramla Bay (via Nadur)	4	6.50
Xagħra	4	6.50
Xlendi Bay	6	9.60

(All distances quoted are approximate)

There are a number of garages where cars and self-drive cars can be hired including Avis Rent-a-Car (Tel. 21225986); Hertz (Tel. 21314636); Wembley (Tel. 21234558 and 21222913) and John's Garage (Tel. 21238745).

Petrol Stations

Petrol stations are open from 6 a.m. to 6 p.m. Mondays to Saturdays. After 6 p.m. and on Sundays and Public Holidays automatic self-service stations are open and payment made at the meters.

Traffic Accidents

If involved in a traffic accident phone the Police (Tel. 112) and, if necessary call for an ambulance (Tel. 112).

Timed Parking Zone

Timed Parking Zones have been introduced in some areas. A parking meter disc is provided and should be used to indicate the time of arrival in any of these zones, and the disc displayed on the dashboard. The vehicle should be removed from the parking space before the expiry of the maximum period indicated.

Festas and Festivals

Those of you who enjoy colour, pageantry and fireworks, with a brass band thrown in, should look out for the "Festas" which are held in towns and villages throughout the two Islands. These are religious festivals with indoor religious services and outdoor celebrations held mainly in the evening during the weekend. The Church is richly decorated, and booths with pastries and sweetmeats are to be found in the streets. There is a brisk trade in "pastizzi" (cheese-cakes), and delicious nougat with honey and almonds.

Festas

There are over fifty *Festas* held each year and the following is a selection giving dates which may coincide with your visit.

Date	*Town or Village*	*Titular Saint*
MALTA		
10th February	Valletta	St Paul's Shipwreck
19th March	Rabat	St Joseph
Sunday nearest to 25th March	Żejtun	St Catherine
1st Wednesday after Easter	Marsaxlokk	St Gregory
4th Sunday after Easter	Balzan	Annunciation

2nd Sunday after Easter	Floriana	St Publius
1st Sunday after Ascension	Qormi	St George
1st Sunday after Ascension	Żurrieq	St Catherine
3rd Sunday in July	Qormi	St Sebastian
1st Sunday in July	Sliema	Our Lady of the Sacred Heart
3rd August	Valletta	St Dominic
15th August	Mosta	Santa Maria
1st Sunday after 18th August	Birkirkara	St Helen
1st Sunday after 15th August	Mġarr	Santa Maria
8th September	Mellieħa	Our Lady of Victories
8th December	Cospicua	Immaculate Conception

GOZO

3rd Sunday in July	Rabat	St George
15th August	Rabat	Santa Maria
8th December	Rabat	Immaculate Conception

Blessing of Animals

An endearing and traditional ceremony takes place outside the Church of Our Lady of Victories, in Valletta, when horses, donkeys, dogs, cats and birds are blessed on the Feast of St Anthony, celebrated in the afternoon on the 1st Sunday after the 16th January. A similar ceremony is held outside the Church of St Augustine in Rabat, in the morning. During the rule of the Order of St John, the Grand Master's carriage drawn by four mules headed the procession of four-legged animals, who received the priest's blessing, bread and a handful of grain.

Good Friday

Good Friday processions are held in the evening in many parts of the Island including Valletta, Rabat, Mosta and Qormi. Similar processions are held in Gozo. These are solemn processions without fireworks and the gaiety which usually accompany other Festas. But there is a great deal of pageantry, with life-size statues and people dressed as "Romans" and "Jews" and acting episodes in the Life and Passion of Our Lord. The Procession often includes masked pentinents carrying crosses, with chains tied to their ankles.

The Christian Information Centre (Tel. 21556210) makes arrangements which enable visitors to watch Good Friday processions from enclosed areas with seating accommodation.

The Last Supper

During Holy Week, at St Dominic's Church in Valletta, and elsewhere, you can see a re-enactment of the Last Supper and in most Churches the traditional ceremony of the Washing of the Feet takes place. Shops and places of entertainment are closed on Good Friday.

Easter Sunday

The Easter Egg is often accompanied by a *figolla*, a sweet made out of special pastry cut to various shapes and covered in marzipan. There is also a traditional early morning "procession", where a statue of the Risen Christ is carried, at speed, through the streets of Qormi and Cospicua on Easter Sunday.

Christmas

Christmas is Christmas everywhere. In the Maltese Islands a characteristic feature is the *Presepju*, a presentation of Christ's birth in the manger in Bethlehem. This takes its place in many homes alongside the Christmas Tree and is often an artistic, and sometimes an elaborate affair. Gifts are, of course, exchanged during Christmas, and the ancient custom of giving presents (*L-Istrina*) on New Year's Day still persists.

The "Imnarja"

This folk festival is held on the night of June 28th (feast of St Peter and St Paul) at Buskett Gardens, which surround Verdala Castle on the outskirts of Rabat. It is usually crowded with people listening to folk music, singing, and eating rabbit washed down with red wine.

Men compete at the ancient singing game of the *għanja*. These are rhyming verses, often extemporised on the spot, and chanted to a traditional lilt and guitar accompaniment, not dissimilar to the flamenco singing of Andalusia in Spain. In the afternoon of June 29th bare-back horse and donkey races are held near Rabat. "L-Imnarja" remains popular, and in the old days it was so important that many brides insisted on including a visit to this festival in the marriage contract. (A visit to Żejtun on the feast of St Gregory and to Valletta on the feast of St John was also included).

Carnival

Carnival is held in many Catholic countries and consists of three days of merrymaking in public with a colourful procession of grotesque masks and decorated cars, with lots of noise and music – a good-natured riot.

It was introduced here with the coming of the Order of St John and it sometimes got out of hand. Grand Master Jean Paul Lascaris, a grim faced Frenchman, tried to control it by forbidding women under pain of the lash to wear masks in public. In return, Maltese women still refer to any churlish fellow as having "*wiċċ Laskri*" – the face of Lascaris. Fancy dress balls are held throughout the Island and the public festivities take place in Valletta and Floriana, and in Gozo.

Traditionally Carnival is held during the three days preceding Ash Wednesday.

Freedom Day, Independence Day and Republic Day

31st March, 21st September and 13th December, respectively. Parades and band marches in Valletta. (See Public Holidays on page 285).

Feast of Our Lady of Victories

8th September. Boat regatta in the Grand Harbour.

Trade Fair

The Malta International Fair is held annually at Naxxar between July 1st and 15th.

Of Things Maltese

Karrozzin – Horse-Drawn Cab

The Maltese horse-drawn cab – *The Karrozzin* – was first introduced into Malta in 1856. Since Queen Victoria was the reigning Monarch at the time, they were at first known as "Victorias". They were the main means of transport until the introduction of the motor car early in this century. Rupert Brooke (1887-1915) who came to Malta shortly before his death wrote: "I drove around in a funny little carriage and looked at the views. It's a lovely place, very like Verona, but rather cleaner and more Southern. There was a lovely Mediterranean sunset, and the sky was filled with colour …"

The 'Karozzin'

The 'Dgħajsa'

The Dgħajsa – Taxi-boat

The *dgħajsa*, (pronounced "dye-sah"), that gaily painted cousin of the Venetian gondola is often the first thing noticed by visitors arriving by sea. Something similar to the *dgħajsa* was probably common in the Grand Harbour in ancient times – the eye of Osiris, God of the Under-World is to this day painted on the bows to ward off the evil eye – but in its present form, it may have been introduced here by the Venetians at the beginning of the sixteenth century. At Kalkara, where this type of boat is made, the *dgħajsa* is still referred to as the "Gondla". Notice that the *dgħajsa*-man pushes rather than pulls his long oars.

Brass Dolphins – Door-knockers

The brass dolphins door-knockers is also characteristic of the Island. The dolphin is a traditional symbol of a seafaring people and it is frequently found on ancient Maltese coins.

The Dolphin was also the emblem of the Langue of Provence and there is a representative mural decoration of it in the chapel of St Michael in St John's Co-Cathedral. Since Independence, two dolphins have formed part of the Island's coat-of-arms.

Hand-made Lace

Hand-made Malta lace – now manufactured mainly on the Island of Gozo – is much sought after. Early in the seventeenth century lace-making was considered a suitable occupation for the well bred women and a century later the art had spread so that there was hardly a village which did not make it. Queen Victoria, in order to encourage the lace-making industry, once ordered a scarf and "eight dozen pairs long and eight dozens pairs short mits".

The Blood Orange

The most celebrated of the Island's fruit tree is the orange. Many thousands of plants have been exported to the Middle East, to North Africa and France (where they are referred to as *maltaises*) as well as to Spain, Italy, South Africa and the United States (especially Florida).

The best oranges grow in the central part of Malta in Lija, Balzan, Attard and Mosta, Żebbuġ and Siġġiewi. There are several varieties including the tasty blood orange, so called because of its blood colour peel and the blood streaks of the pulp. Others are the Bahia orange introduced here by Governor Grenfell in 1901; the egg or Portuguese orange introduced during the Spanish period; the China orange introduced during the rule of the Order of St John and the bitter orange used for making marmalade. From the blossoms of bitter oranges is distilled the "orange-flower water" (*ilma żahar*). The egg-blood orange, which is practically seedless, is probably the best of the lot.

The Maltese Dog

References to the Maltese dog are to be found in the writings of Pliny the Elder (A.D. 23-79) and of Stabo (63 B.C.-A.D. 21) and there is a well-known story that Publius, the chief man of the Island during the time of St Paul's shipwreck, owned a Maltese dog named *Issa* and that he gave a Maltese dog to the Apostle. There is however no evidence for this and the first authentic reference to its existence in Malta is to be found in a book entitled "Ancient and Modern Malta", written in 1805 by Louis de Boisgelin, a French Knight of Malta:

"There was formerly a breed of dogs in Malta with long silky hair, which were in great request in the time of the Romans, but have for some years greatly dwindled ... Aristotle mentions them as being perfectly proportioned notwithstanding their very small size."

The Maltese dog was a great favourite with women both during the Middle Ages and early in the nineteenth century. It is believed they were introduced into England during the reign of Henry VIII (1509-1574) and into the United States around 1874.

The Maltese dog is now rarely seen in Malta but is to be found (either with straight or with curly hair) in many parts of the world including Ireland, Italy, England and the United States.

There is another native dog, somewhat like a miniature greyhound, called *Tal-Fenek*, the "Rabbit Dog", which has bred for centuries and remains very popular with farmers. Also known as the Pharaoh Hound this is claimed to be one of the oldest domesticated dog breeds in the world. The exact origins is debated but one widely held theory is that its origin was in ancient Egypt and that Phoenician traders brought the dog to Malta where it is considered the national dog of the island. Efforts are in hand to encourage the breeding of this dog which is in danger of extinction, at least in its island of origin.

The Wall Clock – "Arloġġ ta' Malta"

The attractive wall clock to be found in several palaces and private homes is of Maltese design and manufacture. The exact period when these clocks were first made is not known, but some still in existence date back to the eighteenth century.

The general design of the Italian altar clock which died out in the early 18th century was revived in Malta. The pioneer is believed to have been Kalċidonju Pisani from the village of Siġġiewi. The design differs from the prototype in that the Maltese clock hangs on the wall instead of standing on a table. Early examples possessed an hour hand only, later ones also had a minute hand.

The clock consists of wooden case and is usually 61 cm long by just over 46 cm wide. The wood is painted in a colour to the liking of the owner – red, blue and green are popular – and the whole clock is heavily gilded and the dial is often decorated with flower designs. Smaller clocks are also made.

Until the outbreak of the First World War the clocks cost a gold sovereign and were sometimes referred to as "arloġġ tal-lira" – "lira" in this case being a gold sovereign. Nowadays, a genuine antique, complete with machinery (also made locally) is hard to come by. An imitation antique can however be ordered, but because of the demand and the time involved in gilding you may have to wait twelve months or more for the finished article, which may be found in some shops including those in Rabat.

The Faldetta – Head-dress

Up the end of the Great War (1914-1918) the head dress of many Maltese women was the *Faldetta*, also known as the *Għonnella*. This consisted of a voluminous hood of rich silk, black everywhere except in Żejtun and Żabbar, where it was usually blue. Some say this garment came into existence as a defence against the excessive gallantry of Napoleon's troops. But this is not so, as the *Faldetta* is of much more ancient origin – prints of the 16th century at the National Library in Valletta testify to this. Nowadays the head dress is rarely if even seen. In his sketch on Malta the Frenchman, Andre Maurois wrote:
'When its wearer moves, the *Faldetta* is filled with air, and the Maltese girls, tripping in twos and threes along the streets, like the flotillas of graceful barques with black sails, blown along their course by the wind of destiny.'

Wooden Balconies

The pervasive closed wooden balcony *Gallarija* is characteristic of Malta and probably dates back to the seventeenth century. (The open stone balcony sometimes found in Mdina and in Għarb, Gozo, is of older vintage).

Many examples are to be found in Old Theatre Street, Valletta and eslewhere, including the President's Palace in Republic Street. Though similar wooden balconies are to be found in other European countries, Italy and Hungary among them, it is in Malta that they are numerous.

In Malta the *gallarija*, possibly related to the Spanish *miradores*, was often furnished with high chairs which allowed the owner to have a clear view of what was happening in the street below, while being sheltered from sun and rain. They are like 'opera boxes' overlooking 'the street of theatre'.

50. A Maltese wall clock

51. An oil painting of a Chicken Hawker by Edward Caruana Dingli (1876-1950)

Ancient Customs

Ancient customs and traditional beliefs contribute towards the identity of a people and the visitor may be interested to learn about some which are peculiar to Malta and Gozo.

Many of these customs are now things of the past, but a few survive. Among these is *Il-Quċċija*, a party given by parents on a child's first birthday.

First Birthday

This is how Boisgelin, writing in 1805, describes *Il-Quċċija*: "The company being met ... the child is brought in; and if it be a boy he is presented with two baskets, coins, and inkstands, a sword etc. The choice he makes on this occasion, will give a just idea of his future disposition, and the mode of life he will embrace. Should he choose the coin, it is a sign of a liberal character, if he prefers the ink-stand, he is to be brought up either to trade or the bar; if he takes the sword, the greatest hopes are entertained of his courage ... If the child is a girl, needles, silks and ribbons, supply the place of the sword and the ink-stand".

Carnival

Another custom, *Il-Kukkanja* held during Carnival and introduced by the Order of St John is also described by Boisgelin: "An entertainment was formerly given on Shrove-Tuesday by the Grand Master to the people, in the great square of the city Valletta. Long beams were fixed against the guardhouse opposite to the Palace, and between each were fastened rope ladders, the whole covered over by branches of trees in leaf: to which were tied from top to bottom, live animals, baskets of eggs, hams, sausages, wreaths of oranges; in short all kinds of provision. The edifice was called *Cocagna* and was crowned by a globe composed of linen cloth on which stood the figure of Fame, *in relievo*, holding a flag with the Grand Master's arms.

"The people were assembled in the great square and were prevented from attacking the Cocagna, till the Grand Master gave the signal ... The provisions of the *Cocagna* became the property of those who, having seized them, were able to carry them off in safety through the crowd. This caused furious battles ... To the first who reached the figure of Fame, was allotted some pecuniary remuneration, and on the standards' being taken to be returned to the Grand Master, the cloth globe, composed of two parts, burst open, and out came a flight of pigeons."

The *Kukkanja* has recently been revived in Malta and is sometimes held in Republic's Square, Valletta, during Carnival.

Folklore

Here are some other ancient customs, traditions and beliefs:

A country lad in search of a wife places a red carnation over his ear and a red handkerchief over his shoulder with one end of the handkerchief in the corner of his mouth.

A father who had marriageable daughters placed pots of Sweet Basil and some Madónna Roses over his front door – one pot of Basil for each marriageable daughter.

When there was death in a household the door-knockers were removed, all mirrors covered with black cloth and no fire lit for three days; food was provided by the neighbours. The women cut their hair and the men go out with unshaven beards. A number of women called *Newwieħa* used to be hired to accompany the corpse. Dressed in long black cloaks they would show appropriate remorse by their cries of lamentation.

Eels are often kept in wells since it is claimed they purify the water.

The horns of a bull or a cow attached over the door give protection against the evil eye.

According to one tradition, St Paul removed the poison from snakes in Malta. Another (rather unkind one) asserts that this poison is now to be found in the tongues of the women!

The water in which a baby has his first bath should have a gold ring in it; in this way riches will come to the child.

Weather Lore (see page 257)

Facts at Your Fingertips

Bus Service

The bus system is inexpensive though not particularly comfortable. The main bus terminus is just outside the City Gate, Valletta and the majority of routes terminate here. Services begin at around 5.30 a.m. and terminate at about 10 p.m. weekdays, at 11 p.m. at weekends. Bus information, see plan on page 282, or ring 21225916.

Gozo's main bus station is in Victoria at Triq Putirjal (Tel. 21556011). In Gozo buses are less frequent and finish earlier than in Malta.

Some Bus routes

IN MALTA

Valletta to	No.
Malta International Airport, Gudja	8
Buġibba	49, 57, 58
Golden Bay	47, 52
Mdina and Rabat	80, 81
Paceville	54, 55, 56
Qawra	49, 57, 15, 449
San Anton Gardens	40, 47, 80, 81
Sliema (Ferries)	61, 62, 64, 67, 68
Sliema (Savoy)	60
St Lukes Hospital	75

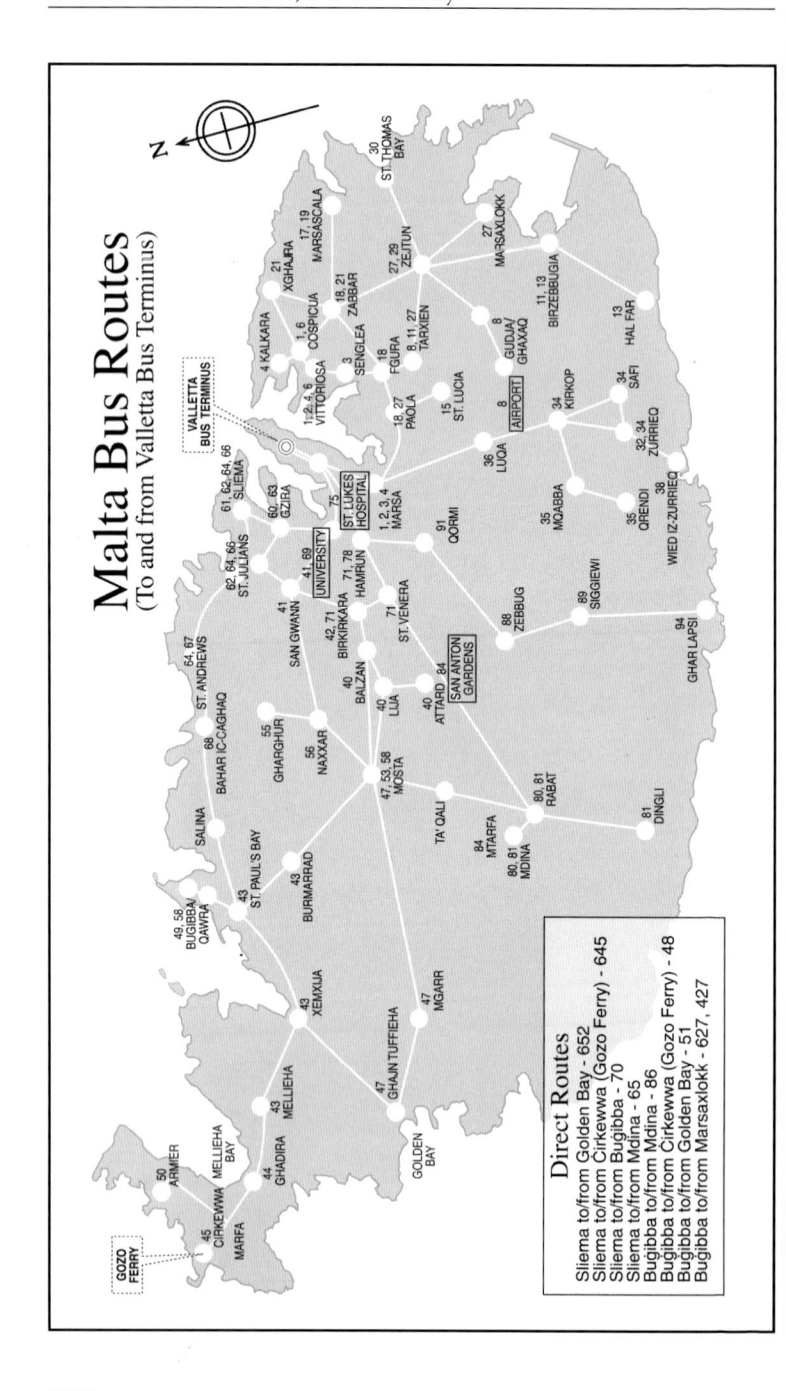

Malta Bus Routes
(To and from Valletta Bus Terminus)

Direct Routes

Sliema to/from Golden Bay - 652
Sliema to/from Cirkewwa (Gozo Ferry) - 645
Sliema to/from Bugibba - 70
Sliema to/from Mdina - 65
Bugibba to/from Mdina - 86
Bugibba to/from Cirkewwa (Gozo Ferry) - 48
Bugibba to/from Golden Bay - 51
Bugibba to/from Marsaxlokk - 627, 427

St Paul's Bay	43, 44, 45, 49, 50, 52, 452
Vittoriosa	1

IN GOZO

From Victoria to

San Lawrenz	2, 91
Sannat	50
Santa Lucia	14
Ta' Pinu	61, 91
Xagħra	64, 65
Xewkija	42, 43
Xlendi	87
Żebbuġ	90, 91

Museums at a Glance

IN MALTA

National Museum of Archaeology, Republic Street, Valletta
National Museum of Fine Arts, South Street, Valletta
National Museum of Natural History, St Publius Square, Mdina
Cathedral Museum, Archbishop Square, Mdina
Wignacourt College Museum, Rabat
Museum and Crypt of St Agatha, Rabat
Ħal Saflieni Hypogeum, Paola
Tarxien Temples, Tarxien
Għar Dalam Cave and Museum, Birżebbugia
Ħaġar Qim & Mnajdra Temples, Qrendi
Maritime Museum, Vittoriosa
Museum of Banking, Bank of Valletta Centre, High Street, Sliema
Manoel Theatre Museum, Valletta

IN GOZO

Museum of Archaeology, The Citadel, Victoria
Folklore Museum, The Citadel, Victoria
Natural Science Museum, The Citadel, Victoria
Malta Aviation Museum, National Park, Ta' Qali
Ta' Kola Windmill, Xagħra
Għarb Folklore Museum, Church Square, Għarb

Banks

Hours of business:

HSBC: 1st October to 14 June, 8.30 a.m. to 12.45, Monday to Friday. 4 p.m. to 8 p.m. on Monday and Thursday and from 4.30 to 7 p.m. on Tuesday and Friday. Saturday, 8.30 a.m. to 12 noon. From June 15 to September 30 branches are open from 8 a.m. to 2 p.m., Monday to Thursday. Fridays from 8 a.m. to 3.30 p.m. Saturday, 8.15 a.m. to 11.30.

Bank of Valletta: 1st October to 14 June, 8.30 a.m. to 2 p.m., Monday to Thursday. On Fridays branches open from 8.30 a.m. to 3.30 p.m. Saturday from 8.30 to 12.30 p.m. From June 15 to September 30 open from 8 a.m. to 2 p.m. Monday to Thursday. In Gozo Bank of Valletta open until 1.15 p.m. On Saturday open from 8.15 to 11.30. Friday all branches including Gozo open from 8 a.m. to 3.30 p.m.

Lombard Bank is located at 67 Republic Street, Valletta and **APS Bank** at 24 St Anne Square, Floriana

VALLETTA

HSBC Bank, 32,34 Merchants Street. (Tel. 21245281)
Bank of Valletta, 45 Republic Street. (Tel. 21244271)
Central Bank of Malta, Castille Place (Tel. 25502000)

SLIEMA – ST JULIANS

HSBC Bank, Airways House, High Street (Tel. 21333096); 112 Manuel Dimech St, Sliema (Tel. 21319229); and St George's Road, St Julians (Tel. 21336467).
Bank of Valletta, The Strand, Sliema (Tel. 21333084)

The Travel Bureau at Gudja International Airport is open 24 hours daily.

MDINA – RABAT

HSBC Bank, Saqqajja Square, Rabat. (Tel. 21454715)
Bank of Valletta, Saqqajja Square, Rabat. (Tel. 21455966)

BUĠIBBA – ST PAUL'S BAY

HSBC Bank, St Paul's Street, St Paul's Bay. (Tel. 21571412)
Bank of Valletta, Islet Promenade, Buġibba. (Tel. 21571749)

GOZO

HSBC Bank, 90 Republic Street. (Tel. 21556266)
Bank of Valletta, Main Square, Victoria. (Tel. 21551113)

All banks are closed on Sunday and on Public Holidays.

Public Holidays

The following days are kept as Public Holidays. On most, though not all of these, shops will be closed. Incidentally, if you are here on business remember that Government Offices close at 1 p.m. from 15th June to 30 September.

January 1: New Year's Day
February 10: Feast of St Paul Shipwrecked
March 19: Feast of St Joseph
March 31: Freedom Day
Variable: Good Friday
Variable: Easter Sunday
May 1: Workers' Day
June 7: 'Sette Giugno'
June 29: Feast of St Peter and St Paul
August 15: Feast of the Assumption
September 8: Feast of Our Lady of Victories
September 21: Independence Day
December 8: Feast of the Immaculate Conception
December 13: Republic Day
December 25: Christmas Day

Airline Agents

		Tel. No.
Air Malta	285 Republic St, Valletta	21240686
Alitalia	MIA, Flr. 2, Luqa	21237115
British Airways	30 Republic Street, Valletta	21242233

Posts, Telephones and Telegrams

Postal Rates – Airmail

United Kingdom & Ireland	16c
France, Germany and Italy	16c
Cyprus & Gibraltar	16c
Spain, Sweden and Switzerland	16c
USA & Canada	22c
Australia	37c

The postal rate for letters to any part of Malta and Gozo is 7c.

International Dialling

Australia: 00672; Austria: 0043; Belgium: 0032; Canada: 001; Eire: 00353; France: 0033; Germany: 0049; Gibraltar: 00350; Israel: 00972; Italy: 0039; Libya: 00218; Russia: 007; Spain: 0034; Sweden: 0046; Switzerland: 0041; Tunisia: 00216; United Kingdom: 0044; and USA: 001.

Internal Telephones

To call the:

Malta International Airport 21249600
Fire Brigade, 112
Telephone faults, 133
Directory enquiries, 1182
Overseas Operator, 1152
Government Information Services, 153
Time check, 195
Emergency air and sea rescue:
  AFM Helicopter section, 112
  AFM Patrol Boat Section, 112

Telecentres

The following offices supply full services, such as local and international telephone calls, and fax services:

Valletta: 28B South Street (Allcom Shop). Telephone 21233354.
Malta International Airport, Telephone 21249382/3.
Gozo, Victoria, Republic Street, Telephone 21563590.

'Mobile Guide'

Signposts have been fixed to several historical buildings quoting a mobile telephone number which when called gives visitors background information, on the building in question.

Taxi Fares

FROM THE AIRPORT

Taxi fares from the Airport to most destinations in Malta may be obtained at the Airport. Here are some of them:

Airport to:

Attard, Lm8
Balzan, Lm8
Birzebbugia, Lm6
Buġibba, Lm10
Ċirkewwa, Lm13
Floriana, Lm6
Golden Bay, Lm10
Marfa, Lm13
Mdina, Lm7
Mosta, Lm9
Paceville, Lm8
Rabat, Lm7
Senglea, Lm7
Sliema, Lm8
St Julians, Lm8
St Paul's Bay, Lm10
Valletta, Lm6

Visitors travelling by taxi from the Airport pay the fare at the ticket boot in the arrivals lounge. A ticket is issued showing the amount paid and the destination; on arrival the ticket is handed to the driver. Any complaints should be addressed to the Public Transport Authority (Tel. 21255165).

Bus. No. 8 takes you to Valletta from the Airport.

Newspapers

Newspapers from the United Kingdom are available either on the morning or in the evening of the day of publication. English language newspapers published in Malta include *The Times* and *The Sunday Times of Malta*, and *The Independent* and *The Independent on Sunday*.

Hospitals

Government General Hospital, St Luke's Gwardamangia, (Tel. 21241251).
Gozo General Hospital, Tel. 21561600
Private Hospitals include: St James (Capua) Hospital, Sliema, (Tel.21335235; 21335240), and
St Philip's Hospital, St Venera, (Tel. 21442211, 21480304)

Nursing

Nursing in the home is provided by the Malta Memorial District Nursing Association (M.M.D.N.A.) Non-members requiring treatment are charged a small fee. (Tel. 21331166, 21331172)

Tourist Information Services

The Malta Tourism Authority is housed at the Auberge d'Italie in Merchants Street, Valletta (Tel. 21224444).

Information and Brochures available at the City Gate, Valletta (Tel. 21237747), and at these Tourist Offices:
Malta International Airport, (Tel. 21249600).
Bay Street, Paceville, (Tel. 21380600).
Mġarr Harbour, Gozo, (Tel. 553343).
Victoria, Gozo, (Tel. 21558106).
In the United Kingdom, Malta House 36-39 Piccadilly, London WIV OPP, (Tel. +44 (0207) 1292 4900).
In Italy, Ente Nazionale per il Turismo di Malta, Via Gonzaga 7, 20123, Milan, (Tel. +39 (02) 8673746).
In France, Office National de Tourisme de Malte, 9 Cite de Trevise, 75009 Paris, (Tel. +33 (1) 48 00 03 79).
In Germany, Office Frankfurt Main, (Tel. +49 069 285890).
United States, 65 Broadway, Suite 823, New York, New York 10006 (Tel. 12124303799).

Learning English

There are over thirty licensed language schools in Malta and Gozo and some 50,000 students come to the islands each year to learn English.

Lists of schools may be obtained from the Tourism Authority in Merchants Street, (Tel. 21224444).

Cultural Activities

The British Council

The British Council is to be found at the British High Commission, Whitehall Mansions, Ta' Xbiex Seafront, Ta' Xbiex (Tel. 23230000).
British Residents Association Magazine. 10 Qronfla, St Patrick Street, Rabat RBT 07. Editor Mr Ken Yale. (Tel.

21459988). General Secretary Ms Mary Attard c/o BRA, PO Box 39, Birkirkara BKR 01 (Tel. 21441891).

Fondazzjoni Patrimonju Malti

Fondazzjoni Patrimonju Malti (Heritage Foundation of Malta) organizes Exhibitions and publishes books and magazines – *Treasures of Malta* – and is housed in Old Bakery Street, Valletta (Tel. 21231515). The Publishing Division is at 86 Old Mint Street, Valletta (Tel. 21228145).

Din L-Art Ħelwa

Din L-Art Ħelwa ('This Fair Land') is a National Association for safeguarding the historic, artistic and natural heritage of the islands. Subscription fee Lm7.50 per annum. 133 Melita Street, Valletta (Tel. 21225952).

St James Cavalier, Centre for Creativity, (Tel. 21223216)

The Italian Cultural Institute

The *Istituto Italiano di Cultura* is at the Palace Square, Valletta. (Tel. 21221462).

Circolo Dante Alighieri

The Circolo Dante Alighieri has a library and organizes cultural activities as well as courses in the Italian language. 134 Old Bakery Street, Valletta (Tel. 21238408).

Alliance Française

The Alliance Française de Malte is at 103, 'Casa Sir L. Preziosi', St Thomas Street, Floriana (Tel. 21238456).

German-Maltese Circle

The German Maltese Circle is to be found at 141 'Messina Place', St Christopher Street, Valletta (Tel. 21246967).

Russian Centre

Russian Cultural Centre is at 36 Merchants Street, Valletta. (Tel. 21222030).

Chinese Cultural Centre

A Chinese Cultural Centre is situated at 173, Melita Street, Valletta (Embassy in St Julians, Tel. 21384698).

Useful Telephone Numbers

Most of the numbers listed below appear elsewhere in this Guide but it may prove useful to group them together for easy reference.

Police 112
Ambulance 112
Fire 112
English Speaking Alcoholics Anonymous Helpline 21579613
Government Information Service 153

Overseas Operator 1152
Time Check 195
Emergency Rescue:
  Helicopter 112
  Patrol Boat 112

Sunday Church Services

Ever since St Paul was shipwrecked in Malta in A.D. 60, Malta and Gozo have been in communion with the Roman Catholic Church and Catholicism has remained very much part of the life of these Islands. Practically all the 380,000 inhabitants are baptized Catholics and there are over 300 churches which are usually full on Sundays and Feast Days.

The Archbishop of Malta, H.G. Mgr. Joseph Mercieca, has selected four priests to care for the spiritual welfare of non-Maltese Catholics either resident in, or on a visit to Malta.

The following are some Sunday Church Services:

VALLETTA – FLORIANA

Roman Catholic

St Barbara, Republic Street, Valletta. 10 a.m. (for French-speaking Catholics), 11 a.m. (German), Noon (English).
St Catherine, Victory Square, Valletta. 11 a.m. (for Italian-speaking Catholics).
St John's Co-Cathedral, St John's Square, Valletta. 7.15 a.m., 8 a.m., 9.15 a.m. (High Mass), Noon, and 5.30 p.m. (Winter), 6 p.m. (Summer).
Greek Catholic Church, Archbishop Str., Valletta, Divine Liturgy at 9 a.m.
St Publius, Floriana, 8 a.m., 9 a.m. (High Mass), 11 a.m. and 6.30 p.m.

Anglican

St Paul's Anglican, Pro-Cathedral, Independence Square, Valletta, 8 and 11.40 a.m. Holy Communion; 10.30 a.m. Matins and Sermon; 6.30 p.m. Evensong and Sermon (Tel. 21225714).

Church of Scotland, Methodist and Free Churches

St Andrew's Scots Church, South Street, Valletta. 10 a.m. (Tel. 21222643).

Greek Orthodox Church

St Gregory's Church, 83 Merchants Street, Valletta. Divine Liturgy of St John Chrysostom at 10 a.m.

Jewish Community

Jewish Community. Secretary (Tel. 21445924)

Buddist Centre

Zen (Buddhist) Centre 24/4 St Ursula Street, Valletta VLT 06. (Tel. 21232059).

SLIEMA – ST JULIANS

Roman Catholic

Stella Maris, High Street, Sliema, 7, 8, 9 (High Mass), 10, 11, Noon and 6.30 p.m.
St Patrick's (For English-speaking Catholics), St John Bosco Street, (Tel. 21334614), 7.30, 9, 10 and 7.30 p.m.

Jesus of Nazareth Church, the Strand, Sliema, 7, 8, (High Mass), 9, 10, 11 and 6.30 p.m. (7 p.m. between 1st April and 30th September).
Carmelite Church, Main Street, St Julians, 7, 8, 9, 10, 11, Noon and 6 p.m.
Mater Boni Consilii, Paceville, St Julians, 8, 9, 10, 11 a.m., Noon and 6 p.m.

Anglican

Holy Trinity Church, Rudolph Street, Sliema (Tel. 21330575), 8 a.m. Communions, 8.45 a.m. Matins, 10.30 a.m. Sung Eucharist, 6.30 p.m. Evensong.

MDINA – RABAT

Roman Catholic

Cathedral, St Paul's Square, Mdina, 7, 8, 9.15 (High Mass), and 11 a.m. (On 1st Fridays 6 p.m.)
St Dominic's, St Dominic's Square, Rabat. 7, 8 (High Mass), 9, 10 and 11.15 a.m. (For English-speaking Catholics).

ST PAUL'S BAY

Parish Church, St Paul's Street, 11 a.m.

ST JULIANS

Casa Leone, (formerly Blue Sisters convent) 11 a.m., and on Sunday at 6 p.m.

BIRZEBBUGIA

St George's Chapel, 10 a.m.

BUĠIBBA

St Maximilian Kolbe Church, 10 a.m.

MARSASCALA

St Anne's, 10 a.m.

MELLIEĦA

Our Lady's Sanctuary, 10 a.m.

TA' XBIEX

Parish Church, 10 a.m.

GOZO

Ecumenical, Enrico Mizzi Street, Victoria. Services in English on first and third Wednesday of each month. 11.15 a.m.
St George's, Rabat, 6, 7, 8, 9, 10, 11 and Noon.
Salesian Sisters Chapel, Republic Street, Rabat. (Mass in English).

FACTS AT YOUR FINGERTIPS

The Language – "Malti"

Pronunciation of Place Names

As mentioned elsewhere in this WELCOME TRAVEL GUIDE most people in Malta understand or speak English and you are unlikely to have any language problems. But place names are a different matter and a few hints on pronunciation will come in useful. The Maltese alphabet is made up to twenty-four consonants and five vowels and it is the consonants that present the greatest difficulty to the visitor. You should note the following:

- ċ with a dot above is soft as in *cheese*
- g is hard as in *game*
- ġ with a dot above is soft as in *gender* (or j as in jam)
- għ is regarded as a single letter and is silent when preceeded or followed by any of the vowels, a, e and o
- h is silent except at the end of a word
- ħ (crossed) is pronounced as in *hard*
- j is pronounced like the English *y*
- m is pronounced *im* when the initial letter is followed by a consonant, e.g. Mdina is pronounced *Im-dee-na*
- x is pronounced *sh* as in shore
- z is hard and is pronounced *ts*
- ż with a dot above is soft as in *zero*

Place Names

IN MALTA

Baħrija	*Bah-ree-ya*
Comino	*Co-me-no*
Għajn Tuffieħa	*Eye-n-Two-fee-ha*
Għar Dalam	*Ar-dalam*
Gudja	*Good-ya*

297

Ħaġar Qim	*Hajar-Qem*
Kunċizzjoni	*Koon-chits-joh-nee*
Lija	*Lee-ya*
Marsamxett	*Marsam-chet*
Marsaxlokk	*Marsa-shlock*
Mellieħa	*Mel-lee-ha*
Mdina	*Im-dee-na*
Mtaħleb	*Im-tah-leb*
Mnajdra	*Im-nigh-dra*
Salina	*Sa-lee-na*
Selmun	*Sel-moon*
Sliema	*Slee-ma*
Ta' Xbiex	*Ta Shbeesh*
Wardija	*War-dee-ya*
Wied Iż-Żurrieq	*Weed-ezz-zoo-reek*

IN GOZO

Dwejra	*Dway-ra*
Daħlet Qorrot	*Dahlet Or-rot*
Għarb	*Arb*
Gozo	*Go-tzo*
Ġgantija (Temple)	*Gee-gun-tee-ya*
Mġarr ix-Xini	*Im-jar ish-shee-nee*
Qala	*Ah-la*
Qawra	*Aw-ra*
Ta' Pinu	*Ta Pi-noo*
Xagħra	*Sha-ra*
Xlendi	*Shlen-dee*

Useful Words

Yes	Iva (*ee-va*)
No	Le (as in lemon)
When?	Meta? (*mett-ah*)

Now	Issa (*iss-sah*)
Please	Jekk jogħġbok (*yek-yoj-bock*)
Thank You	Grazzi (*grats-tsee*)
How Much?	Kemm?
Good	Tajjeb (*tie-yep*)
Bad	Ħażin (*ha-zeen*)
Show me	Urini (*oo-ree-nee*)
I beg your pardon	Skużi (*skoo-zee*)
Do you speak English?	Taf titkellem bl-Ingliż (*taaf tit-kell-lemm bil-inn-gleez?*)
Pound	Lira (*Lee-ra*)
I want to go to Mdina	Irrid immur l-Imdina (*ir-reet imm-moor lim-dee-na*)
Good Morning	Bonġornu (*bonn-jorr-noo*)
Good Evening	Bonasira (*bonn-a-see-ra*)
Goodbye	Saħħa (*sah-ha*)

Embassies/Diplomatic Representation in Malta

Australia

The Australian High Commission, Villa Fiorentina, Ta' Xbiex Terrace, Ta' Xbiex MSD 11 (Tel. 21338201)

Britain

The British High Commission, Whitehall Mansions, Ta' Xbiex Seafront, Ta' Xbiex, (Tel. 23230000). Passport and Consular enquiries Tel. 23232234.

China
Embassy of the People's Republic of China, Karmnu Court, Lapsi Street, St Julians (Tel. 21384695).

Egypt

Embassy of the Arab Republic of Egypt, Villa Mon Reve, 10, Sir Temi Zammit Street, Ta' Xbiex MSD 11 (Tel. 21314158).

France

Embassy of France, 130, Melita Street, Valletta, P.O.Box 408, Valletta (Tel. 21233430).

Federal Republic of Germany

Embassy of the Federal Republic of Germany Il-Pjazzetta Building, Tower Road, Sliema. P.O.Box 48, Marsa (Tel. 21336520).

Holy See

Apostolic Nunciature of Malta, "Villa Cor Jesu", Tal-Virtu Road, Tal-Virtu, Rabat (Tel. 21453422).

Israel

Embassy of Israel, Via Michele Mercati 34, 00187, Rome, Italy. (Tel. 0039-06-361785.00).

Italy

Embassy of Italy, 5, Vilhena Street, Floriana VLT14 (Tel. 21233157).

Libya

Embassy of The Peoples Bureau of the Great Socialist Libyan arab Jamahiriyea. Notabile Road, Balzan BZN 01 (Tel. 21486347).

Order of St John

Sovereign Military Hospitaller Order of St John of Jerusalem, of Rhodes and of Malta, St John's Cavalier, Ordinance Street, Valletta VLT 11 (Tel. 21223670).

Russia

Embassy of The Russian Federation, Briel House, Anthony Schembri Street, Kappara, San Gwann (Tel. 21371905).

Tunisia

Embassy of Tunisia, 144/2, Tower Road, Sliema (Tel. 21332182).

United States of America

Embassy of the United States of America, Development House, St Anne Street, Floriana, P.O.Box 535, Valletta (Tel. 21235960).

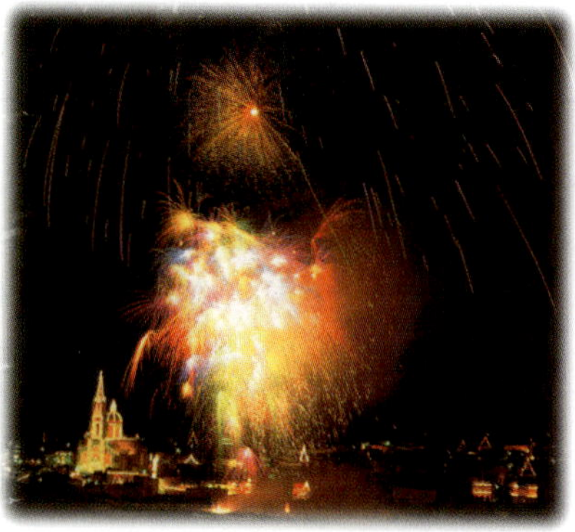

Further Reading

BIANCHI, P., and SERRACINO INGLOTT P. (Editors), *Encounters with Malta* (2000)
BONELLO, GIOVANNI, *Art in Malta – Discoveries and Recoveries* (1999)
BRADFORD, ERNLE, *The Great Siege* (1961)
BLOUET, BRIAN, *The Story of Malta* (1984)
BROCKMAN, ERIC, *Last Bastion* (Re-print 2002)
BROOKES R. and ALDEN S., *Malta, New Climbs* (1986)
CARUANA GALIZIA, ANNE and HELEN, *The Food & Cookery of Malta* (1997)
CASSAR, PAUL, *Medical History of Malta* (1965)
CAVALIERO, RODERICK, *The Last of the Crusaders* (Re-print 2001)
DE PIRO, NICHOLAS, *The International Dictionary of Artists Who Painted Malta* (2003)
DE VERTOT, ABBE, *History of the Knights of Malta* (1728)
ENGLAND, RICHARD, *Walls of Malta* (1972)
FARRUGIA, JIMMY, *Antique Maltese Domestic Silver* (1992)
HUGHES, QUENTIN, *The Buildings of Malta 1530-1795* (1956); *Fortress Architecture and Military History in Malta* (1969); *Fortress, Architecture and Military History in Malta* (Re-print 2001)
LAFERLA, ALBERT, *The Story of Malta* (1935); *British Malta* (1938)
LUKE, SIR HARRY, *Malta, An Account and an Appreciation* (1960)
MANDUCA, JOHN, (Editor), *Antique Furniture in Malta* (2002)
MIDDLETON, NED, *Maltese Islands – Diving Guide* (1997)
PEROWNE, STEWART, *The Siege Within the Walls* (1970)

RYAN, FREDERICK, *Malta* (1910)
SCHERMERHORN, ELIZABETH, *Malta of the Knights* (1929)
SCICLUNA, SIR HANNIBAL, *The Church of St John in Valletta* (1955)
SPITERI, STEPHEN, *Fortresses of the Knights* (2001)
TRUMP, DAVID, *Prehistory and Temples* (2002)
ZAMMIT, SIR THEMISTOCLES, *Malta, the Islands and their History* (1929)

Appendices

SOVEREIGNS FROM 1090 TO 1530

NORMANS:

Roger (Count of Normandy)	1091-1101
Simon (Son of Count Roger)	1101
Roger II (Son of Count Roger)	1101-1154
William I (Son of Roger II)	1154-1166
William II (Son of William I)	1166-1189
Tancred I (Son of Roger II)	1189-1194
William III (Son of Tancred I)	1194

SUABIANS:

Constance (Daughter of Roger II and wife of Henry VI of the House of Hohenstaufen)	1194-1197
Frederick I (Son of Constance)	1197-1250
Conrad I (Son of Frederick I)	1250-1254
Conradin (Son of Conrad I)	1254-1266
Manfred (Natural son of Frederick I)	1266

ANGEVINS:

Charles of Anjou	1266-1283

ARAGONESE:

Peter I (III of Aragon)	1283-1285
James I (Son of Peter I)	1285-1296
Frederick II (Son of Peter I)	1296-1337

Peter II (Son of Frederick II)   1337-1342
Louis I (Son of Peter II)   1342-1355
Frederick III (Son of Peter II)   1355-1377
Mary I (Daughter of Frederick III)   1377-1420
Martin I (Husband of Mary I)   1402-1409
Martin II (Son of Martin and Mary)   1409-1412

CASTILLIANS:

Ferdinand I (Nephew of Martin II)   1412-1416
Alphonso I (Son of Ferdinand I)   1416-1458
John I (Son of Ferdinand I)   1458-1479
Ferdinand II (Son of John I)   1479-1516
Joanna I (Daughter of Ferdinand II)   1516-1518
Charles (Son of Joanna and Philip of Austria,
    Emperor of the Holy Roman Empire)   1518-1530

GRAND MASTERS OF THE ORDER OF ST JOHN IN MALTA

Philippe Villiers de L'Isle Adam (French)	1530-1534[1]
Pietro del Ponte (Italian)	1534-1535
Didier de Saint Jaille (French)	1535-1536
Juan de Homedes (Spanish)	1536-1553
Claude de la Sengle (French)	1553-1557
Jean Parisot de la Valette (French)	1557-1568
Pietro del Monte (Italian)	1568-1572
Jean l'Eveque de la Cassiere (French)	1572-1581
Hughes Loubenx de Verdalle (French)	1581-1595
Martin Garzes (Spanish)	1595-1601
Alof de Wignacourt (French)	1601-1622
Luis Mendez de Vasconcellos (Portuguese)	1622-1623
Antoine de Paule (French)	1623-1636
Jean Paul de Lascaris Castellar (French)	1636-1657
Martin de Redin (Spanish)	1657-1660
Annet de Clermont de Chattes Gessan (French)	1660
Rafael Cotoner (Spanish)	1660-1663
Nicolas Cotoner (Spanish)	1663-1680
Gregorio Carafa (Italian)	1680-1690
Adrien de Wignacourt (French)	1690-1697
Ramon Perellos y Roccaful (Spanish)	1697-1720
Marc' Antonio Zondadari (Italian)	1720-1722
Antonio Manoel de Vilhena (Portuguese)	1722-1736
Ramon Despuig (Spanish)	1736-1741
Manoel Pinto de Fonseca (Portuguese)	1741-1773
Francisco Ximenes de Texadas (Spanish)	1773-1775
Emmanuel de Rohan Polduc (French)	1775-1797
Ferdinand de Hompesch (German)	1797-1798

---

[1] In Rhodes from 1521.

CIVIL COMMISSIONERS, GOVERNORS and GOVERNORS-GENERAL

CIVIL COMMISSIONERS

Captain Alexander Ball, R.N.	1799-1801
Major-General Henry Pigot	1801
Sir Charles Cameron	1801-1802
Vice-Admiral Sir Alexander Ball, Bart.	1801-1802
Lieutenant-General Sir Hildebrand Oakes	1810-1813

GOVERNORS

Lieutenant-General the Honourable Sir Thomas Maitland	1813-1824
General the Marquess of Hastings	1824-1826
Major-General the Honourable Sir Frederick Ponsomby	1827-1836
Lieutenant-General Sir Henry Bouverie	1836-1843
Lieutenant-General Sir Patrick Stuart	1843-1847
The Right Honourable Richard More O'Ferrall	1847-1851
Major-General Sir William Reid	1851-1858
Lieutenant-General Sir John Gaspard le Marchant	1858-1864
Lieutenant-General Sir Henry Storks	1864-1867
General Sir Patrick Grant	1867-1872
General Sir Charles Van Straubenzee	1872-1878
General Sir Arthur Borton	1878-1884
General Sir Lintorn Simmons	1884-1888
Lieutenant-General Sir Henry Torrens	1888-1890
Lieutenant-General Sir Henry Smyth	1890-1893
General Sir Arthur Fremantle	1893-1899
Lieutenant-General Lord Grenfell	1889-1903
General Sir Mansfield Clarke, Bart.	1903-1907
Lieutenant-General Sir Henry Grant	1907-1909
General Sir Leslie Rundle	1909-1915

Field-Marshal Lord Methuen	1915-1919
Field-Marshal Viscount Plumer	1919-1924
General Sir Walter Congreve	1924-1927
General Sir John du Cane	1927-1931
General Sir David Campbell	1931-1936
General Sir Charles Bonham-Carter	1936-1940
Lieutenant-General Sir William Dobbie	1940-1942
Field-Marshal Viscount Gort	1942-1944
Lieutenant-General Sir Edmond Schreiber	1944-1945
Sir Francis Douglas (later Lord)	1945-1949
Sir Gerald Creasy	1949-1954
Major-General Sir Robert Laycock	1954-1959
Admiral Sir Guy Grantham	1959-1962
Sir Maurice Dorman	1962-1964

GOVERNORS-GENERAL

Sir Maurice Dorman	1964-1971
Sir Anthony Mamo	1971-1974

MALTA and GOZO – Sun, Sea and History

PRESIDENTS

Sir Anthony Mamo	1974-1977
Dr. Anton Buttigieg	1977-1982
Miss Agatha Barbara	1982-1987
Mr Paul Xuereb (acting)	1987-1989
Dr Vincent Tabone	1989-1994
Dr Ugo Mifsud Bonnici	1994-1999
Professor Guido de Marco	1999-

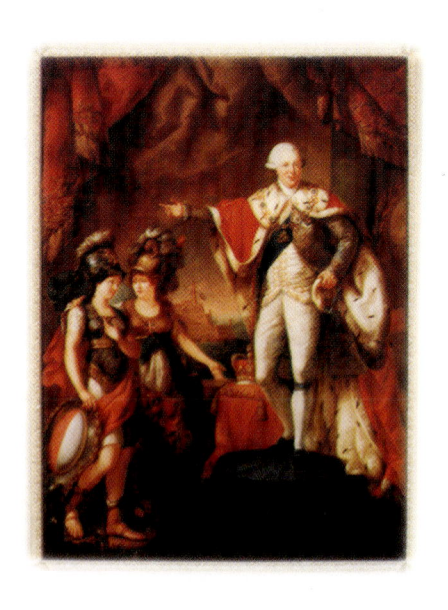

PRIME MINISTERS OF MALTA

Senator Joseph Howard	1921-1923
Dr. Francesco Buhagiar	1923-1924
Sir Ugo Mifsud	1924-1927
Sir Gerald (later Lord) Strickland, Count della Catena	1927-1932
Sir Ugo Mifsud	1932-1933
Dr. (later Sir) Paul Boffa	1947-1950
Dr. Enrico Mizzi	1950 (Sept.-Dec.)
Dr. Giorgio Borg Olivier	1950-1955
Mr. Dom Mintoff	1955-1958
Dr. Giorgio Borg Olivier	1962-1971
Mr. Dom Mintoff	1971-1984
Dr Carmelo Mifsud Bonnici	1984-1987
Dr. Edward Fenech Adami	1987-1996
Dr. Alfred Sant	1996-1998
Dr. Edward Fenech Adami	1998-2003
Dr. Edward Fenech Adami	2003-

Index

A

Abercromby, General Sir Ralph, 66
Adelaide, Dowager Queen, 62
Airline Agents, 286
Alfonso XIII, King of Spain, 93
Alexander VII, Pope, 172
Alitalia, 286
Alemagne, Auberge d', 60
American Naval Squadron, 40
Angevins, 34
Anglican Cathedral, Valletta, 153
Animals, Blessing of, 266
Apiary, Roman, 38
Arabs, the, 34
Archives, National, 94, 108
Archaeological Sites & Temples, 121
Archbishop's Palace, Mdina, 100
Archbishop's Palace, Valletta, 62
Argotti Botanic Gardens, 139
Armier Bay, 250
Armoury, Palace, 58
Auberges, 60, 173
Audio-Visual Shows, 240
Aviation, Museum, 179

B

Bahrija, 284
Ball, Sir Alexander, 38
Banks, 284
Balconies, wooden, 275
Baviere, Auberge de, 62
Barracca, Lower, 137
Barracca, Upper, 136
Bathing, *see* Swimming
Bay Street Complex, 238
Bighi, Villa, 175
Bingemma, Fort, 134
Blue Grotto, 178

Boisgelin, Louis de, 274
Bologna, Family, 89
Bonaparte, Lucien, 143
Bonaparte, Napoleon, 38
Books on Malta, 303
Brass Dolphins, 271
Bread, Maltese, 230
British, the, 38
British Airways, 286
British Council, 290
British High Commission, 299
British rule, 38-42
Brooke, Rupert, 270
Bugibba, 176
Buses, 281
Bus route, 282
Bush, President George, 110
Buskett Gardens, 143
Byron, 39

C

Cab, horse-drawn, 270
Calypso, 191
Caravaggio, 51
Carnival, 268
Carmelite Church, Mdina, 98
Cart-ruts, 125
Carthaginians, the, 32
Casa Bernard, Rabat, 101
Casa Rocca Piccola, Valletta, 59
Casino Maltese (Private Club), 53
Cassar, Girolamo, 60
Castilians, 34
Castello, Gozo, 192
Catacombs, Rabat, 107
Celini, Benevento, 96
Cemeteries, 145
Chadwick 'Lakes', 186

Chapelle, family, 89
Chemists, 247
Charles V of Aragon, 35
Cheese, Maltese, 229
Church Services, 293
Churchill, Sir Winston, 41
Cinemas, 239
Circolo Dante Aligieri, 291
Citta Vecchia, (See Mdina)
Cliffs & Countryside, 182
Climate, 255
Clocks, Maltese, 274
Clothing, 28
Cloth, Malta weave, 245
Coleridge, Samuel Taylor, 43
Comino, Island of, 206
Cottoner Lines, 131, 184
Crafts, 243
Crimea, 39
Cultural Activities, 290
Currency, 26
Customs, 26
Customs, ancient, 278

D

Depiro Family, 89
Dghajsa, taxi-boat, 271
Dingli Cliffs, 110
Din l-Art Helwa, 291
Disraeli, 38
Disco/Nightclubs, 240
Diving Site, 248
Dogs, Maltese, 273
Dragut, 193

E

Eating Out (Malta), 227
Eating Out (Gozo), 237
Edward VII, King, 41, 70
Elizabeth, Queen, 41, 137
Embassies, 298
Entertainment, 238

F

Falcon, Maltese, 36
Faldetta, see Head-Dress
Ferdinand, King of Naples, 187
Festas, 265

Filfla, island of, 111
Fish, Mediterranean, 228
Folklore, 278
Food, Maltese, 227
Forts & Fortifications, 129, 134
Fondazzjoni Patrimonju Malti, 291
France, Auberge de, 60
France, Embassy of, 300
French rule, 38
Fruit, Maltese, 229
Fungus Rock, Gozo, 201

G

Gambling Casinos, 239
Gardens, 136
Garibaldi, 39
George V, King, 41
George VI, King, 41
George Cross, 40
Germany, Embassy of, 300
German-Maltese Circle, 292
Ggantija Temples, Gozo, 196
Ghar Dalam, 125, 187
Golf, 251
Good Friday Processions, 267
Gorbachev, President, 110
Governors, British, 308
Gozo, 189-208
Gozo-Malta Ferry service, 205
Graham, Colonel, 187
Greek Catholic Church, 64
Grand Masters, 307
Grognet de Vase, Giorgio 176
Guides, licensed, 260

H

Hagar Qim, temples, 123
Halls of Montezuma, 40
Hal Millieri Chapel, 179
Hamilton, Lady, 188
Harbour, Grand, 168
Harbour, Tours, 253
Hasan's Cave, 181
Hastings Gardens, 138
Head-Dress, Maltese, 275
Helicopter Service, 205
'Heritage in Stone', 179
Highlights – Must Do, 52

INDEX

Holidays, Public, 285
Holy See, 300
Honey, 33
Horse Racing, 252
Hospital of the Order, 69
Hospitals, 289
Hotels, 220
Hypogeum, 121

I
Ice Arena, 238
Inguanez Family, 93
Innocent XII, Pope, 172
Inquisitor's Summer Palace, Girgenti, 110
Inquisitor's Palace, Vittoriosa, 171
Israel, Embassy of, 300
International Telephones, 287
Italian Cultural Institute, 291
Italian Embassy, 300

J
Jesuit Church, Valletta, 68
Jewish Cemeteries, 146
Johnson, Dr, 38

K
Karrozzin, see Cab,
Kennedy, Memorial Grove, 113
Kukkanja, 278

L
La Valetta, Grand Master, 37
Lace, 272
Lear, Edward, 39
Library, National, 54
Libya, Embassy, 301
Licensing hours, 29

M
Maglio Gardens, 138
'Malta Experience', 70, 240
Malta House, London, 290
Maltese Cross, 37
Maltese Language, 297
Manduca Antonio, 175
Manduca Family, 89
Manoel Theatre, Valletta, 59

Markets, open air, 247
Mdina, 89
Medieval Hamlet, 111
Mediterranean Conference Centre, 69
Mellieha sanctuary, 150
Merchants Street, Valletta, 66
Methodist Church, 294
Mnajdra temples, 123
Monastic Orders, 35
Mosta Church, 176
Moscati Parisio family, 100
Motoring, 261
Museums, 202, 283
Museum of Archaeology, 48
Museum, Aviation, 179
Museum, Cathedral, Mdina, 97
Museum of Fine Arts, Valletta, 47
Museum, Maritime, 173
Museum, Natural History, Mdina, 91
Museum, St John's, Valletta, 53
Museum, War, 66
Museum, Wignacourt College, 105
Mustapha, Pasha, 37

N
Nature Reserve, 181
Nelson, Lord, 188
Newspapers, 289
Nobility, Maltese, 89
Normans, 34
'Norman House', Mdina, 98
Notabile: see Mdina

O
Opera House, Valletta, 47
Oranges, Maltese, 272
Order of St John, 35
Our Lady of Damascus, 64

P
Palace, Grand Masters, Valletta, 55
Paul, Saint, 149
Parisio, Palazzo, Naxxar, 144
Palazzo Parisio, Valletta, 68
Passports, 26
'Petticoat Lane', 68
Philip, Prince, 41
Phoenicians, 32

Pius VII, Pope, 54
Pius IX, Pope, 142
Postal rates, 286
Preti, Mattia, 51
Provence, Auberge de,
Public Holidays, 285
Public Registry, Valletta, 68

Q
Qawra, 176, 199
Quccija, 276

R
Rabat, 101
Restaurants, Gozo, 232
Restaurants, Malta, 227
Rinella, Fort, 134
Rinella Movie Park, 181
Roger of Normandy, 34
Roman House, Rabat, 101
Romans, 32
Roosevelt, FDR, 41
Royal Malta Artillery, 65

S
Sailing, 252
St Agatha's Chapel, Mdina, 92
St Agatha's Crypt, Rabat, 107
St Angelo, Fort, 169
St Benedict's Nunnery, Mdina, 92
St Dominic, Priory, Rabat, 108
St Elmo, Fort, Valletta, 65
St James Cavalier, Valletta, 291
St John's Co-Cathedral, Valletta, 48
St Julian's, 71
St Lawrence, Church, Vittoriosa, 172
St Nicholas, Mdina, 99
St Patrick's Church, Sliema, 294
St Paul's Anglican Church, 62
St Paul's Church and Grotto, Rabat, 104, 148
St Paul's Island, 151
St Publius, Church, Floriana, 46
San Anton Gardens, Attard, 142
San Blas Bay, Gozo, 203
San Dimitri, Gozo, 191
Santa Maria Bay, Comino, 206
Santo Spirito Hospital, Rabat, 108

Saura Old People's Home, Rabat, 108
Shopping, 244
Siege-Bell Memorial, 70
Sliema, 71, 222
Soleyman, the Magnificent, 37
Spaniards, the, 34
Spinola Palace, 71
Sports, 249
Stalactite caves, Gozo, 199
Starkey, Sir Oliver, 53
Strickland, Lord, 96
Swimming, 202, 249

T
Tapestry Chamber, Valletta, 57
Ta' Pinu Basilica, Gozo, 197
Tarxien, Temples, 123
Taxis, 288
Temples, prehistoric, 121, 196
Tipping, 29
Tourism Authority, Malta, 43
Tourist Information, 30
Trollope, Anthony, 39

U
Union Club, Sliema, 55
United States, Embassy, 301
University, 69

V
Valletta, 43
Verdala Castle, 109
Victoria, Queen, 54
Victoria Lines, 134, 185
Victoria Melita, Princess, 143
Vilhena Palace, Mdina, 91
Visas, 26
Vittoriosa, 167

W
Walking in Gozo, 203
Walking in Malta, 185
Wall Clock, 274
War Rooms, Lascaris, 71
Weather, 255
Wied iz-Zurrieq, 'The Blue Grotto', 177
Windmills, 201

Wignacourt Museum, Rabat, 105
Wignacourt Tower, 131

X
Xewkija Church, Gozo, 198

Y
Yachting, 252

Z
Zammit, Sir Themistocles, 125

NOTES: